THE MEDITERRANEAN DIET MADE SIMPLE

Discover 120 Delicious Recipes for a Healthier You: Create Nourishing Meals and Achieve Your Health Goals with Ease

Unlock Your Free Wellness Bundle!

Congratulations, on finding your gateway point to a world of empowerment, motivation, and holistic well-being. Delve into our treasure trove of Freebies crafted to enhance all aspects of your life from mind, body, and soul. Are you prepared to embark on a journey of transformation? Let's get started!

Transform your life with our exclusive freebies:

Holistic Wellness Guide Ebook: Radiant Living Made Simple. **Mediterranean Delights Ebook:** Delectable recipes for your soul.

To access your **Bonus**, scan the QR code below:

Contents

INTRODUCTION

When we think of a "diet" these days, we usually think of some kind of restriction that will help us achieve a certain goal, such as losing weight. The Mediterranean diet is the polar opposite of that. Rather, it promotes a diet that comprises the food staple of people who live in Mediterranean nations such as Spain, Greece, Italy, and France. It also emphasizes community when dining- think dinners with family and friends and great discussion.

Mediterranean dieters stress a plant-based eating style rich in vegetables and healthy fats, such as olive oil and omega-3 fatty acids from fish, in their meals. It's a well-known, heart-healthy diet.

Vegetables and fruits, whole grains, fish, nuts and legumes, and olive oil are all abundant in this diet. This diet limits or eliminates red meat, sugary foods, and dairy (however, small amounts of yogurt and cheese are permitted).

Eating this way leaves little room for processed foods. When you look at a plate, it ought to be full of traditional proteins, such as chicken, maybe more of a side dish than the main attraction, which is produce.

The Mediterranean diet's tolerance of low to moderate amounts of red wine is something that many individuals appreciate. "Moderate" indicates 5 ounces (oz) or less per day (about one glass). It's worth emphasizing, though, that a daily glass of wine is not required on this diet, and if you don't already drink, this allowance isn't a reason to start.

This book contains 120 of my favorite hand-picked Mediterranean recipes. The meals you create will be very delicious. Promise!

All of the recipes in this book are rather easy to prepare and are written in a clear and straightforward manner. You won't have to worry about what to do next since these recipes will lead you every step of the way to making the most delicious Mediterranean meals ever. You don't believe me when I say they're that good? Let these recipes prove themselves. Enjoy!

CHAPTER ONE

OVERVIEW OF MEDITERRANEAN DIET

It's likely that you have heard of the Mediterranean diet. If you suffer from a chronic condition like heart disease or high blood pressure, your doctor may have suggested it to you.

The Mediterranean diet, which is high in vegetables, fruits, whole grains, and heart-healthy fats, is both delicious and has health benefits. It can aid with weight management, heart health, and the prevention of diabetes.

Researchers first became interested in the Mediterranean diet in the 1950s, when some populations in the Mediterranean Sea bowl were found to have better overall health, lower rates of cardiovascular and metabolic diseases, and greater longevity than wealthier Western nations. Thus, the diet denotes the traditional food traditions of the Mediterranean Sea's surrounding countries, which include Greece, Italy, Spain, Morocco, Egypt, and Lebanon. Vegetables and fruits, whole grains, seafood, nuts and legumes, and olive oil are all staples of the Mediterranean diet. Poultry, eggs, cheese, and dairy are consumed in smaller quantities. The Dietary Guidelines for Americans (DGA) promote the Mediterranean diet as a "healthy dietary pattern." However, unlike many fad diets, this one stresses eating nutrient-dense foods rather than tracking calories or altogether avoiding any one food type.

Furthermore, the Mediterranean diet covers more than just food; as a result, it is often referred to as a way of life. People in Mediterranean regions have traditionally prioritized physical activity, social gatherings, and leisure, as well as moderate consumption of wine with meals. In the United States, moderate alcohol consumption is defined as two drinks or less per day for men and one drink or fewer per day for women. One drink equals 1.5 ounces of 80-proof (or 40%) distilled spirits or liquor, 12 ounces of 5% alcohol beer, or 5 ounces of 12% alcohol wine.

Unlike many other popular eating patterns, the Mediterranean diet is designed to be easily adaptable to a variety of cuisines and preferences. It is a manner of eating that emphasizes appreciating whole foods and frequent physical exercise rather than a strict meal plan. Here, we give you the benefits of the Mediterranean diet and a blueprint for following it.

HOW DOES THE MEDITERRANEAN WORK?

The Mediterranean diet is a diet that was developed to mimic the typical eating habits of the countries surrounding the Mediterranean Sea. You don't have to reside in Spain, Italy, or France to benefit from the eating pattern; many individuals are switching to it because of the numerous health benefits it gives. And more and more research is revealing that foods from all over the world (rather than just one specific location) can provide the same advantages when consumed in amounts similar to those in the Mediterranean diet.

The Mediterranean diet is linked to lower cholesterol, a lower chance of Alzheimer's and Parkinson's disease, a lower risk of heart disease, and a longer life. According to new research, it may also lessen the risk of, and maybe help those suffering from, anxiety, depression, type 2 diabetes, and several malignancies.

The Mediterranean diet is not a strict diet. It is, rather, a manner of eating that promotes fruits and vegetables, whole grains, legumes, and healthy plant-based oils. Fish is the primary protein source instead of red meat, pork, or chicken. And, yes, red wine is included—in moderation. Fermented dairy is consumed on a daily basis, but in moderation. Red meat and highly processed foods are occasionally consumed, while eggs and fowl are rarely consumed.

POTENTIAL BENEFITS OF A MEDITERRANEAN DIET

The Mediterranean diet has been linked to a slew of health benefits, which include the following:

Aids in weight loss

Following a Mediterranean diet has not been proven to cause weight loss in studies. However, studies have shown that it may be a suitable long-term alternative for people trying to lose weight.

According to studies, people who followed the diet for 5 years were less likely to develop excess weight than those who followed alternative diets.

Among the advantages are:

- Having a wide variety implies that the diet is not restrictive and hence easy to follow.
- High fiber levels indicate that a person is more likely to feel content for longer periods of time and is less inclined to nibble.
- Healthy fats are less likely to induce obesity-related cardiac issues.

Improves cardiac health

The American Heart Association recommends the Mediterranean diet as an evidence-based approach to avoiding cardiovascular disease and stroke.

Some researchers, for example, compared the benefits of the Mediterranean diet to those of a low-fat diet in 2021. The Mediterranean diet, they determined, was more successful at reducing the advancement of plaque accumulation in the arteries. Plaque accumulation is a significant risk factor for heart disease.

Another study found that the Mediterranean diet may benefit heart health by decreasing blood pressure.

Maintains healthy blood sugar levels

The Mediterranean diet can help in the prevention of type 2 diabetes and the stabilization of blood sugar levels. According to research, it can:

- Lower fasting blood glucose levels
- Raise hemoglobin A1C levels, a test used to assess long-term glucose levels.
- Minimize insulin resistance, which prevents the body from adequately using insulin to manage blood sugar levels.

It safeguards brain function.

The Mediterranean diet can improve brain health and help prevent cognitive loss as you age. According to studies, there may be a link between following a Mediterranean diet, greater memory, and lower levels of many risk factors for Alzheimer's disease.

In addition, a major review found that the Mediterranean diet improved cognitive function, memory, attention, and processing speed in healthy older people.

GETTING STARTED WITH THE MEDITERRANEAN DIET

When in doubt, remember this basic fraction rule: Make half of your dish fruits and vegetables, one-quarter whole grains, and one-quarter healthy protein. The Mediterranean diet is purposefully vague about specific foods, focusing instead on dietary groups to include so that it can be adjusted to different types of cuisine and flavor preferences. Here are some more suggestions for filling those gaps:

Emphasis on Whole Foods

The Mediterranean diet does not often include highly processed foods. Review the ingredient list if it comes in a package. When possible, choose foods that contain only whole-food ingredients such as nuts, legumes, or whole grains such as oats and bulgur. Fruits, vegetables, fish, and healthful plant-based oils like olive oil are all examples of whole foods.

Make vegetables the focus of your meal.

Fruits and vegetables should make up most of your meals. The Mediterranean diet advocates seven to ten servings of fruits and vegetables daily; however, research indicates that three to five servings can lower the risk of cardiovascular disease. Think of simple ways to include more vegetables in your diet, such as adding spinach to your eggs or heaping your sandwich with avocado and cucumber. As an alternative to crackers, try unsweetened yogurt with frozen berries, eating an apple with nut butter, mixed nuts, or oatmeal with dried fruit as a snack.

Replace red meat with fish.

The major sources of protein in the Mediterranean diet are fatty fish like mackerel, salmon, tuna, and herring. These fish have significant omega-3 fatty acid concentrations, which help in the reduction of inflammation and the improvement of cholesterol levels. Furthermore, if you don't have access to fresh fish, canned versions are just as nutritious, easier to prepare, and stay much longer in your cupboard. White fish and shellfish are also rich sources of lean protein but not as abundant in omega-3s. Red and highly processed meats are consumed infrequently and should be reserved for exceptional occasions. Turkey, chicken, eggs, cheese, and yogurt can be eaten on a daily or weekly basis, but in moderation.

Instead of butter, cook with plant-based oil.

Healthy plant-based oils, such as olive oil, are the major sources of fat in the Mediterranean diet. Total fat isn't as significant as fat type. The Mediterranean diet promotes the consumption of heart-healthy fats (polyunsaturated and monounsaturated fats) while avoiding saturated and trans fats. Unsaturated fat is found in oils such as canola oil, olive oil, avocado oil, sesame oil, peanut oil, and sunflower oil.

When consumed in excess, trans and saturated fats can raise LDL ("bad") cholesterol. To help lower your cholesterol and enhance your heart health, replace butter with heart-healthy fats such as plant-based oils high in unsaturated fat.

Reconsider your dairy.

Instead of topping everything with higher-saturated-fat dairy products like heavy cream or cheese, seek to consume a range of tasty cheeses or dairy products (particularly fermented dairy products) in moderation. Choose strong-flavored cheeses, such as feta or Parmesan, where a smaller amount can provide the desired flavor, and aim to restrict your intake of highly processed cheeses, like American.

Enjoy yogurt as well, but when possible, pick plain, fermented, and Greek varieties. Skip the flavored yogurts with a lot of added sugar; too much added sugar might be bad for your health over time.

Whole grains should be used instead of refined grains.

Replace refined grains such as white rice, pasta, and white bread with whole grains like brown rice, corn, quinoa, barley, bulgur, and farro. Whole grains are essential to the Mediterranean diet and have numerous advantages ranging from lowering cholesterol to stabilizing blood sugars and encouraging healthy weight maintenance. Whole grains are also high in fiber and B vitamins.

Beans and legumes have similar health advantages and are likewise included in the Mediterranean diet.

Snack on Nuts

Don't be afraid of the fat found in nuts. Nuts, like plant-based oils and avocados, are high in poly- and monounsaturated fats, which are good for your heart. They are also high in protein and fiber. Fat, protein, and fiber are the ideal combination for feeling full, maintaining blood sugar stability, lowering cholesterol, and reducing inflammation. To add extra to your day, snack on a quarter cup of almonds between lunch and dinner. Most omega-3s are found in walnuts; however, other nuts also contain beneficial fats. If you need more to keep you full, pair them with a fruit or vegetable.

Avoid Added Sugar (Most of the Time)

Highly processed dessert foods such as cookies, crackers, refined flour, and sugar are not common in the Mediterranean diet. However, this does not mean they are completely off-limits. Instead, reserve larger portions of cookies and ice cream for rare occasions. Alternatively, eat naturally sweet foods such as fruit to help fulfill sugar cravings.

Red wine should be consumed in moderation.

That equates to around 5 ounces (or one glass) for women and 10 ounces (or two glasses) for men per day. If you don't drink now, these findings should not be seen as a reason to start.

BREAKFAST RECIPES

CHAPTER TWO

BREAKFAST RECIPES

If you're looking for breakfast ideas for the Mediterranean diet, look no further. Use these healthy meals that are high in fiber to start your morning. Fresh fruits, whole grains, and vegetables, which are easy to include in breakfast meals, are key components of the Mediterranean diet. Here, you can find everything from savory frittatas loaded with vegetables to quick, cozy oatmeal.

1. Egg Sandwiches with Rosemary, Tomato & Feta

Prep Time: 5 minutes

Cook Time: 15 minutes

Serves: 4

Beverage Paring: Lemon water

These filling breakfast sandwiches are stuffed with Mediterranean-inspired ingredients, including feta, tomato, and spinach. We cook eggs in olive oil flavored with delicious rosemary to give them a flavor boost. Olive oil and freshly chopped rosemary are cooked together to enhance the aromatic properties of the rosemary. The rosemary olive oil is used to cook eggs until the whites are set on both sides.

- 4 teaspoons olive oil
- 4 multigrain sandwich thins
- ½ teaspoon dried rosemary, crushed or 1 tablespoon snipped fresh rosemary
- 2 cups fresh baby spinach leaves
- 1 medium tomato, sliced thin into 8
- 4 eggs
- 4 tablespoons reduced-fat feta cheese
- Freshly ground black pepper
- ⅛ teaspoon kosher salt

1. Turn on the 375°F oven. Sandwich thins should be split; brush the sliced sides with 2 teaspoons of olive oil. Put on a rimmed baking sheet and toast for 5 minutes or until the edges are lightly golden and crunchy.

2. In the meantime, heat the rosemary and the remaining two tablespoons of olive oil in a skillet over medium-high heat. One at a time, crack eggs into the skillet. Cook for approximately a minute, or until the yolks are still runny but the whites are set. Use a spatula to crack the yolks. Cook the eggs until done on the other side by flipping them. Get rid of the heat.

3. On 4 serving plates, arrange the bottom halves of the toasted sandwich thins. Sandwich thins on platters should all have spinach on them. Add 2 tomato slices, one egg, and 1 tablespoon of feta cheese to the top of each. Add a little pepper and salt to taste. Add the last of the thin sandwich halves on top.

NUTRITION FACTS (PER SERVING)

Calories: 242	Carbohydrates: 25g	Fat: 12g	Protein: 13g

2. Date & Pine Nut Overnight Oatmeal

Prep Time: 10 minutes

Serves: 1

REFRIGIRATE: OVERNIGHT

These overnight oats are naturally sweetened with chopped dates, honey, and cinnamon, and each bite is balanced by pine nuts.

- ½ cup water
- ½ cup old-fashioned rolled oats
- Pinch of salt
- 1 tablespoon toasted pine nuts
- ¼ teaspoon ground cinnamon
- 2 tablespoons chopped dates
- 1 teaspoon honey

1. In a jar or bowl, mix together the salt, water, and oats. Cover and refrigerate overnight.

2. Oats can be heated or eaten cold in the morning, as desired. Add dates, pine nuts, honey, and cinnamon to the top.

Tips

- A word of advice: Because oats are often contaminated with wheat and barley, those who have gluten sensitivity or celiac disease should only use oats that are marked "gluten-free."
- To prepare ahead, measure, toast, and chop the topping ingredients while preparing the oats the night before.

NUTRITION FACTS (PER SERVING)

Calories: 282	Carbohydrates: 48g	Fat: 9g	Protein: 7g

3. Mozzarella, Basil & Zucchini Frittata

Prep Time: 20 minutes

Serves: 4

Beverage Paring: Green tea

This recipe for a veggie-packed frittata is one of the quickest meals you can cook. Serve it with a small slice of crusty bread drizzled with olive oil and a tossed salad for breakfast, lunch, or dinner, depending on when you make it.

- 1 ½ cups thinly sliced red onion
- 2 tablespoons extra-virgin olive oil
- 1 ½ cups chopped zucchini
- ½ teaspoon salt
- 7 large eggs, beaten
- ¼ teaspoon freshly ground pepper
- 3 tablespoons chopped soft sun-dried tomatoes
- Baby fresh mozzarella balls (about 4 ounces) or ⅔ cup pearl-size
- ¼ cup thinly sliced fresh basil

1. Put the rack in the upper third of the oven and heat the grill.

2. In a sizable nonstick or cast-iron skillet that is safe for broiling, heat oil over medium-high heat. Cook the onion and zucchini for 3 to 5 minutes, stirring regularly, until tender.

3. In the meantime, combine the salt, pepper, and eggs in a bowl. Pour the eggs over the veggies in the saucepan. Cook for about two minutes, raising the edges to let the middle's raw egg pour below. Place the skillet in the grill for 2 to 3 minutes or until the eggs are slightly browned. Sprinkle mozzarella and sun-dried tomatoes over the top. Observe for three minutes. Add basil on top.

4. To remove the frittata from the pan and onto a cutting board or serving tray, use a spatula to work around the frittata's edge and then underneath the pan. Serve after slicing into four pieces.

NUTRITION FACTS (PER SERVING)

Calories: 292	Carbohydrates: 8g	Fat: 21g	Protein: 18g

4. Fig & Ricotta Overnight Oats

Prep Time: 10 minutes

Serves: 1

You can prepare a quick yet filling, fruity, and healthy breakfast the night before with a little effort. You can "cook" these overnight oats while you sleep. Toast the almonds and chop the figs the night before so that you can quickly stir in the figs, almonds, honey, and ricotta cheese for a filling, sweet, and creamy breakfast when you wake up.

- ½ cup water
- ½ cup old-fashioned rolled oats
- Pinch of salt
- 2 tablespoons chopped dried figs
- 2 teaspoons honey
- 2 tablespoons part-skim ricotta cheese
- 1 tablespoon toasted, sliced almonds

1. In a jar or bowl, mix together the salt, water, and oats. Cover and refrigerate overnight.

2. Oats can be heated or eaten cold in the morning, as desired. Add ricotta, figs, almonds, and honey to the top.

Tips

- Oats are often contaminated with barley and wheat; thus, anyone with gluten sensitivity or celiac disease should buy oats that are labeled "gluten-free."
- To prepare ahead of time: When preparing the oats, the previous evening, measure, toast, and chop the topping ingredients.

NUTRITION FACTS (PER SERVING)

Calories: 294	Carbohydrates: 48g	Fat: 9g	Protein: 10g

5. Spinach & Egg Scramble with Raspberries

Prep Time: 10 minutes **Serves:** 1

This quick egg scramble with substantial toast is one of the best meals for weight reduction. It combines filling whole-grain toast, protein-packed eggs, and superfood raspberries with nutrient-dense spinach. You feel fuller and more energetic throughout the morning thanks to protein and fiber.

- 1 ½ cups baby spinach
- 1 teaspoon canola oil
- 2 large eggs, lightly beaten
- Pinch of ground pepper
- ½ cup fresh raspberries
- Pinch of kosher salt
- 1 slice of whole-grain bread, toasted

1. Use a small nonstick skillet with medium-high heat to heat the oil.

2. Add the spinach and boil for 1 to 2 minutes, stirring often, until wilted.

3. Transfer the spinach onto a platter. Clean the pan, then add eggs and cook it up over medium-low.

4. Cook for one to three minutes, stirring once or twice to ensure even cooking. Add the salt, pepper, and spinach, and stir.

5. Serve the scramble along with bread and strawberries.

NUTRITION FACTS (PER SERVING)

Calories: 296	Carbohydrates: 21g	Fat: 16g	Protein: 18g

6. Vegetable Omelets

Prep Time: 30 minutes

Serves: 4

Beverage Paring: Fresh orange juice

It is possible to make the ideal omelet, and this recipe makes it easy to do so! Just start by whisking together the eggs and cream, dicing and sautéing the vegetables, and then making the omelet. Faster than you can say "vegetable omelet," it just takes 10 minutes to cook. Eat this vegetable omelet for dinner or breakfast. For a complete meal, serve it with potatoes or a piece of toast.

- ½ cup cucumber, chopped and seeded
- ½ cup no-salt-added diced tomatoes with garlic, basil, and oregano, well-drained
- ½ cup chopped yellow summer squash
- 2 eggs
- ½ ripe avocado, peeled, pitted, and chopped
- 1 cup frozen or refrigerated egg product, thawed
- 1 teaspoon dried basil, crushed
- 2 tablespoons water
- ¼ teaspoon salt
- 1 Snipped fresh chive
- Nonstick cooking spray, e.g., olive oil
- ¼ teaspoon ground black pepper
- ¼ cup shredded minimized-fat Monterey Jack cheese with jalapeño chile peppers

1. To make the filling, combine the tomatoes, cucumber, squash, and avocado in a medium bowl. Place aside. Mix the eggs, egg substitute, water, basil, salt, and pepper in a medium bowl.

2. Olive oil should be liberally applied to an 8-inch nonstick skillet for each omelet. Over medium heat, warm the skillet. Pour a liberal 1/3 cup of the egg mixture into the hot skillet.

3. Begin stirring the eggs immediately with a wooden spatula in a gentle, continuous motion until the mixture resembles cooked egg bits surrounded by liquid eggs. Stop stirring. Cook the egg for a further 30 to 60 seconds, or until it is set but glossy.

4. Spoon half a cup of the filling over one side of the omelet. Omelet should be carefully folded over the filling. Take off the omelet from the skillet very carefully. To make a total of 4 omelets, repeat the process, wiping the skillet clean with paper towels and spraying it with olive oil in between each omelet. Each omelet should have 1 tablespoon of cheese on it. Add chives as a garnish if preferred.

NUTRITION FACTS (PER SERVING)

Calories: 128	Carbohydrates: 7g	Fat: 6g	Protein: 12g

7. Berry Chia Pudding

Prep Time: 5 minutes

Serves: 2

Beverage Paring: Black coffee

⊙ REFRIGIRATE: OVERNIGHT

Chia seeds include fiber, iron, and calcium, in addition to being a good source of beneficial omega-3 fatty acids. Here, the chia seeds are combined with a fruity base and chilled until the chia seeds swell to create a thick, creamy consistency resembling tapioca.

- 1 cup of almond milk (unsweetened) or any milk of your choice
- 1 ¾ cups blackberries, diced mango (fresh or frozen), and/or raspberries divided
- ¼ cup chia seeds
- ¼ cup granola
- ¾ teaspoon vanilla extract
- 1 tablespoon pure maple syrup
- ½ cup whole-milk plain Greek yogurt

1. Blend or process milk and 1 1/4 cups of fruit until completely smooth. Mix chia, syrup, and vanilla after scraping into a medium bowl. Cover and refrigerate for at least eight hours and up to three days.

2. Layer each serving of pudding with 1/4 cup of the remaining fruit, 1/4 cup of yogurt, and 2 tablespoons of granola. Divide the pudding into 2 dishes.

NUTRITION FACTS (PER SERVING)

Calories: 343	Carbohydrates: 39g	Fat: 15g	Protein: 14g

8. Honey-Roasted Cherry & Ricotta Tartine

Prep Time: 20 minutes

Serves: 4

This simple tartine recipe is ideal for a nutritious breakfast because it features fresh cherries and a creamy ricotta spread that has thyme added. For a quick breakfast or light lunch, serve with a green salad.

- 1 tablespoon honey, plus more for serving
- 2 cups pitted fresh cherries
- 1 teaspoon lemon zest
- 2 teaspoons extra-virgin olive oil
- 1 tablespoon lemon juice
- salt
- 1 cup part-skim ricotta cheese
- 4 whole-grain artisan breads (1/2 inch thick)
- 1 teaspoon fresh thyme
- flaky sea salt, such as Maldon
- ¼ cup slivered almonds, toasted

1. Set the oven to 400 degrees Fahrenheit (2040C). Make use of parchment paper to line a baking sheet with a rim.

2. Mix honey, lemon juice, oil, and salt with the cherries. Roast the cherries on the preheated pan for about 15 minutes, shaking the saucepan once or twice throughout cooking.

3. Griddle bread. Ricotta cheese, lemon zest, roasted cherries, thyme, almonds, and sea salt are garnishes that go on top. If desired, drizzle with extra honey.

NUTRITION FACTS (PER SERVING)

Calories: 320	Carbohydrates: 40g	Fat: 13g	Protein: 14g

9. Berry-Almond Smoothie Bowl

Prep Time: 10 minutes

Serves: 1

This Berry Almond Smoothie Bowl is a tasty meal full of pure and nutritious ingredients. It is smooth and creamy. When you're short on time, having this quick and delicious breakfast is a terrific way to start your morning. Despite being so light, it will keep you satisfied until lunch. And after eating it, you feel fantastic!

- ½ cup frozen sliced banana
- ⅔ cup frozen raspberries
- ½ cup plain unsweetened almond milk
- ¼ teaspoon ground cinnamon
- 5 tablespoons sliced almonds, divided
- ⅛ teaspoon ground cardamom
- ¼ cup blueberries
- ⅛ teaspoon vanilla extract
- 1 tablespoon unsweetened coconut flakes

1. Blend the following ingredients in a blender: banana, raspberries, almond milk, cinnamon, 3 tablespoons of almonds, cardamom, and vanilla. Blend until extremely smooth.

2. The remaining 2 tablespoons of almonds, 2 tablespoons of coconut, and blueberries should be added to the smoothie before serving.

NUTRITION FACTS (PER SERVING)

Calories: 360	Carbohydrates: 46g	Fat: 19g	Protein: 9g

10. Blueberry-Banana Overnight Oats

Prep Time: 10 minutes

Serves: 1

The tastiest overnight oats are made from regular oatmeal when it is combined with blueberries, a sweet banana, and creamy coconut milk. Prepare up to four jars at once and store them in the refrigerator for easy grab-and-go breakfasts all week.

- ½ cup old-fashioned oats
- ½ cup unsweetened coconut milk beverage
- ½ tablespoon chia seeds (optional)
- 1 teaspoon maple syrup
- ½ banana, mashed
- Pinch of salt
- 1 tablespoon unsweetened flaked coconut (optional)
- ½ cup fresh blueberries

1. In a pint-sized container, whisk together the coconut milk, oats, banana, maple syrup, salt, and chia seeds (if using). If desired, add blueberries and coconut to the top. Cover and refrigerate overnight.

NUTRITION FACTS (PER SERVING)

| Calories: 285 | Carbohydrates: 57g | Fat: 6g | Protein: 6g |

vg **gf**

11. Homemade Plain Yogurt

Prep Time: 30 minutes

Serves: 4

Beverage Paring: Herbal Infusions such as mint or chamomile tea

Making yogurt at home is easier than you would think. Four cups of low-fat or nonfat milk and 1/4 cup of low-fat or nonfat yogurt are required for this recipe. Make sure it's one you enjoy because the flavor of the plain yogurt you use in the method will meld with your homemade yogurt. A thermometer and a jar with a lid that holds 5 to 8 cups are also required.

- ¼ cup nonfat or low-fat plain yogurt
- 4 cups nonfat or low-fat milk

1. In a large saucepan, boil the milk over medium-high heat, often stirring, until it steams, barely bubbles, and a candy or instant-read thermometer reads 180 degrees F. (Don't leave it unattended; it will quickly boil over.)

2. Carefully pour the milk into a 5- to 8-cup, clean, heat-safe container. Stirring constantly, let stand until temperature reaches 110 degrees F. In a small bowl, combine the yogurt with 1/2 cup of the 110-degree milk. Stir the yogurt mixture back into the warm milk.

3. To keep the container warm, wrap it in a clean kitchen towel and cover it. Place in a fairly warm location and leave undisturbed for at least 8 hours and maybe up to 12 hours, or until thickened and tangy. 2 hours or so in the fridge will make it chilly. The yogurt will get somewhat thicker in the refrigerator.

NUTRITION FACTS (PER SERVING)

Calories: 137	Carbohydrates: 19g	Fat:	Protein: 14g

12. Muffin-Tin Spanakopita Omelets

Prep Time: 20 minutes

Cook Time: 30 minutes

Serves: 6

These baked eggs take their flavors and textures from spanakopita, a pie of Greek origins that contains eggs, spinach, onion, feta, and crispy phyllo. There is no need to slice and portion these when you are on the move in the morning because they are muffin-size rather than pie-size.

- ⅓ cup finely chopped red onion
- 3 tablespoons extra-virgin olive oil, divided
- ¼ teaspoon salt, divided
- 1 (10-ounce) package of frozen chopped spinach, thawed and squeezed dry
- 6 large eggs
- ½ cup crumbled feta cheese
- 8 sheets phyllo (9-by-14-inch), thawed
- ¼ cup chopped fresh dill
- ½ cup reduced-fat milk
- ½ teaspoon ground pepper

1. Set the oven to 350 degrees Fahrenheit (1760C). Spray extra-virgin oil in a 12-cup muffin pan sparingly.

2. In a pan, preheat 1 tablespoon of oil over medium heat. Add onion and 1/8 teaspoon salt; stir-fry for 4 minutes or until the onion begins to brown. Get rid of the heat. Allow it to cool for five minutes.

3. In a big bowl, mix eggs, spinach, feta, milk, dill, pepper, remaining 1/8 teaspoon salt, and cooked onions.

4. Arrange phyllo sheets on a dry, spotless work surface. (While you put the cups together, cover the sheets with a dish towel to prevent them from drying out.) Place the 2 tablespoons of oil that are left in a small bowl. A clean cutting board should have a sheet of phyllo on it. Apply oil with a light brush. A second sheet of phyllo should be placed on top and lightly brushed with oil. Phyllo is divided into 6 pieces by cutting it in half horizontally and in thirds vertically. Put one square inside each muffin cup, pushing it into the edges and bottom. In order to cover the sides of the muffin cup, add another square while switching up its position. Follow the same procedure with the remaining squares, phyllo sheets, and oil.

5. Squeeze a scant 1/4 cup of the egg mixture into each phyllo cup. Bake for 25 to 30 minutes, or until the phyllo is gently browned and the filling feels firm to the touch.

NUTRITION FACTS (PER SERVING)

Calories: 266	Carbohydrates: 18g	Fat: 16g	Protein: 12g

vg

13. Fig & Ricotta Toast

Prep Time: 5 minutes

Serves: 1

Ricotta toast is an easy and cozy snack. You can create a seasonal breakfast that is both elegant and simple by adding figs, prosciutto, a honey drizzle, and some good salt to the ricotta toast. Here is the perfect recipe for ricotta fig toast.

- ¼ cup part-skim ricotta cheese
- 1 slice crusty whole-grain bread (1/2-inch thick)
- 1 fresh fig or 2 dried, sliced
- 1 teaspoon honey
- 1 teaspoon sliced almonds, toasted
- Pinch of flaky sea salt, e.g., Maldon

1. Toast the bread. Add ricotta cheese, figs, and almonds as garnish. Drizzle with honey; sprinkle with sea salt.

NUTRITION FACTS (PER SERVING)

Calories: 252	Carbohydrates: 32g	Fat: 9g	Protein: 13g

14. Cherry-Walnut Overnight Oats

Prep Time: 10 minutes

Serves: 1

REFRIGIRATE: OVERNIGHT

This overnight oats recipe has a cheesecake-like flavor and creamy texture thanks to cream cheese, dried cherries, and crunchy walnuts. Fresh lemon zest gives the dish a little zip, and a touch of sweetness from raw cane sugar softens the fruit's tartness.

- 1/4 cup of old-fashioned oats
- 1/4 cup water
- Pinch of salt
- Cherries (for garnish)
- Cream cheese (for garnish)
- Walnuts (for garnish)
- Lemon zest (for garnish)
- Sugar (for garnish)

1. In a jar or bowl, whisk together the oats, water, and salt. Cover and refrigerate overnight.

2. You can choose to eat the oats warm or cold in the morning. Cherries, cream cheese, walnuts, lemon zest, and sugar are added as a garnish.

NUTRITION FACTS (PER SERVING)

Calories: 324	Carbohydrates: 46g	Fat: 12g	Protein: 9g

15. Yogurt with Blueberries & Honey

Prep Time: 5 minutes

Serves: 1

Greek yogurt and blueberries are a simple combination that is given a little more sweetness by golden honey. It has the ideal ratio of protein to fiber to keep you feeling energized.

- ½ cup blueberries
- 1 cup nonfat plain Greek yogurt
- 1 teaspoon honey

1. Yogurt should be put in a bowl. Add blueberries on top and sprinkle honey over them.

NUTRITION FACTS (PER SERVING)

Calories: 196	Carbohydrates: 25g	Fat: 1g	Protein: 24g

16. Tomato & Feta Quiche with Spaghetti Squash Crust

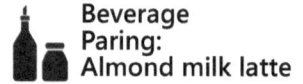

Prep Time: 40 minutes

Cook Time: 1hr 10 minutes

Serves: 6

Beverage Paring: Almond milk latte

Have you ever substituted spaghetti squash for the crust of a low-carb quiche? In this nutritious breakfast meal, roasted spaghetti squash is chopped up and used to make a delightfully crisp quiche crust.

- 1 tablespoon extra-virgin olive oil
- 1 medium spaghetti squash, seeds removed, halved lengthwise
- ¼ teaspoon salt
- 1 large egg, lightly beaten
- ¼ teaspoon pepper
- 2 tablespoons grated Parmesan cheese

Fillings

- ⅔ cup crumbled feta cheese
- 2 large Roma tomatoes, chopped
- 4 large eggs
- 1 cup low-fat milk
- 1 tablespoon sour cream
- ¼ cup chopped fresh parsley
- ¼ teaspoon salt
- 2 teaspoons chopped fresh thyme
- ⅛ teaspoon ground pepper

1. To prepare the crust: Set the oven to 400 degrees Fahrenheit (2040C). Each squash half's cut side should be brushed with oil before being sprinkled with 1/4 teaspoon each of salt and pepper. Squash halves should be placed cut-side down on a rimmed baking sheet and baked for 40 to 50 minutes, or until soft. (Alternatively, put the squash halves, cut-side down, in a pan that can be heated in a microwave while adding 2 tablespoons of water. 10 minutes on High, covered in the microwave, until the flesh is soft.) Scoop off the flesh from each squash half when it is cool enough to handle. (You should consume 4 cups of squash.)

2. Squeeze the squash to extract as much juice as you can by wrapping it in cheesecloth or a tea towel. Spray extra-virgin oil in a 9-inch deep-dish pie pan. Squash, one egg, and Parmesan are combined in a medium bowl. Transfer the mixture to the saucepan and press evenly into the bottom. About 25 minutes into baking, the crust should be firm and starting to color around the edges.

3. To make the quiche's filling and bake it: Sprinkle feta and tomatoes evenly on the crust. Eggs and sour cream should be well mixed. Add salt, pepper, milk, parsley, and thyme by whisking. Pour the egg mixture over the remaining filling ingredients. Lower the oven's setting to 350 degrees Fahrenheit (1760C). Bake the quiche for 30 to 40 minutes, or until the filling is set in the center and starting to color slightly. Before serving, allow it to cool somewhat.

NUTRITION FACTS (PER SERVING)

Calories: 201	Carbohydrates: 15g	Fat: 12g	Protein: 11g

17. Quinoa & Chia Oatmeal Mix

Cook Time: 10 minutes

Serves: 12

Use this nutritious recipe to make your own hot cereal mix. Keep it on hand, and only prepare what you need when you want a hot breakfast. The heated cereal has six grams of fiber per serving, or approximately a fourth of your daily requirement.

- 1 cup rolled wheat and/or barley flakes
- 2 cups old-fashioned rolled oats
- ¾ teaspoon salt
- 1 cup quinoa
- ½ cup chia and/or hemp seeds
- 1 cup dried fruit, e.g., cranberries, raisins, and/or chopped apricots
- 1 teaspoon ground cinnamon

1. To prepare the dry mix for hot cereal: In an airtight container, mix oats, wheat and/or barley flakes, quinoa, dried fruit, seeds, cinnamon, and salt.

2. To prepare 1 cup of hot cereal: In a small saucepan, mix 1 1/4 cups water (or milk) with 1/3 cup Quinoa & Chia Oatmeal Mix. Let it boil. Lower the heat, cover partially, and boil for 12 to 15 minutes until thickened, stirring occasionally. Allow to stand for five minutes, covered. Add your preferred sweetener after stirring, and then, if you like, sprinkle with nuts and/or extra-dried fruit.

NUTRITION FACTS (PER SERVING)

Calories: 196	Carbohydrates: 36g	Fat: 4g	Protein: 6g

18. Avocado-Egg Toast

Prep Time: 5 minutes

Serves: 1

Beverage Paring: Pomegranate juice

Once you give it a try, we think you'll agree that adding an egg to avocado toast makes for almost the ideal breakfast.

- ¼ teaspoon ground pepper
- ¼ avocado
- ⅛ teaspoon garlic powder
- 1 tablespoon scallion, sliced (optional)
- 1 large egg, fried
- 1 slice whole-wheat bread, toasted
- 1 teaspoon Sriracha (optional)

1. Gently mash the avocado in a small bowl while adding pepper and garlic powder.

2. Add a fried egg and the avocado mixture on toast. If desired, garnish with scallion and Sriracha.

NUTRITION FACTS (PER SERVING)

Calories: 271	Carbohydrates: 18g	Fat: 18g	Protein: 12g

19. Breakfast Naan Pizza

Prep Time: 10 minutes

Cook Time: 10 minutes

Serves: 1

This recipe is for you if you're seeking a quick weekend breakfast that your entire family will love! In fact, it's so easy to make that you could do it on a weekday morning. If you're making bacon and scrambled eggs anyway, using them as a topping for naan pizza hardly adds any extra time. Additionally, it's incredibly simple to modify to your tastes and the tastes of your family, and you could even set up a "make your own naan breakfast pizza" bar for a fun brunch party!

- 2 tablespoons part-skim ricotta cheese
- Ground pepper and chopped fresh basil for garnish
- 1 whole-wheat naan
- 1 tablespoon low-sodium marinara or pesto
- 1 large egg
- ½ teaspoon lemon zest
- 1 tablespoon grated Parmesan cheese

1. Set the oven to 425 °F (2180C). Spray cooking oil on a baking sheet with a rim.

2. Naan should be put on the ready pan. In a small bowl, combine the ricotta, marinara (or pesto), and lemon zest. Spread the mixture over the naan to make a well in the center. Crack the egg into the well with care. Add a sprinkle of Parmesan. Bake for 8 to 10 minutes, or until the cheese is melted and the naan is brown. If desired, add basil and pepper as a garnish.

NUTRITION FACTS (PER SERVING)

Calories: 458	Carbohydrates: 52g	Fat: 17g	Protein: 24g

20. Mango-Almond Smoothie Bowl

Prep Time: 10 minutes

Serves: 1

Use frozen fruit (not fresh) for this nutritious smoothie bowl recipe to maintain the thick, creamy, and frosty texture.

- ½ cup nonfat plain Greek yogurt
- ½ cup frozen chopped mango
- ¼ cup frozen sliced banana
- 5 tablespoons unsalted almonds, divided
- ¼ cup plain unsweetened almond milk
- ⅛ teaspoon ground allspice
- ½ teaspoon honey
- ¼ cup raspberries

1. Mango, yogurt, banana, almond milk, 3 tablespoons of almonds, and allspice should all be thoroughly blended in a blender.

2. Place raspberries, the remaining 2 tablespoons of almonds, and honey on top of the smoothie in a bowl.

NUTRITION FACTS (PER SERVING)

Calories: 457	Carbohydrates: 46g	Fat: 24g	Protein: 22g

21. Strawberry & Yogurt Parfait

Prep Time: 10 minutes

Serves: 1

Beverage Paring: Sparkling water with citrus

For a quick breakfast, try this strawberry parfait dish, which mixes fresh fruit, Greek yogurt, and crunchy granola. For a nutritious breakfast on the go, place the parfait in a Mason jar.

- 1 teaspoon sugar
- ¼ cup granola
- 1 cup sliced fresh strawberries
- ½ cup nonfat plain Greek yogurt

1. In a small bowl, mix the strawberries and sugar. Let the berries rest for about 5 minutes or until the berries begin to release juice.

2. To assemble the parfait, put the yogurt in a 2-cup container with the strawberries and their juice. Add granola on top.

NUTRITION FACTS (PER SERVING)

Calories: 285	Carbohydrates: 37g	Fat: 8g	Protein: 17g

22. California-Style Breakfast Sandwich

Prep Time: 10 minutes

Serves: 1

With just a few ingredients, this breakfast sandwich on a bagel tastes freshly made and is ready in no time. A substantial, healthful meal with multiple layers of flavor is created by combining creamy avocado with crisp onions and sprouts.

- 1 everything bagel thin, toasted
- 1 tablespoon roasted garlic avocado-oil mayonnaise
- 1 slice Monterey Jack cheese
- 2 tablespoons thinly sliced red onion
- 2 tablespoons alfalfa sprouts
- ¼ avocado, sliced
- 1 large egg, fried

1. Mayonnaise should be spread on one bagel's thin half. Cheese, avocado, sprouts, a fried egg, and onion go on top. Add the remaining thin bagel half on top.

NUTRITION FACTS (PER SERVING)

Calories: 492	Carbohydrates: 30g	Fat: 36g	Protein: 19g

23. English Muffin Pizza with Tomato & Olives

Prep Time: 5 minutes

Serves: 1

Beverage Paring: Iced herbal hibiscus tea

This English muffin with pizza-inspired toppings, including tomato, cheese, olives, and oregano, serves three purposes: it's fantastic as a snack and also makes a delectable breakfast or lunch.

- 1 medium tomato, sliced
- 1 whole-wheat English muffin, split and toasted
- 1 tablespoon sliced green olives
- ⅛ teaspoon dried oregano
- 2 tablespoons shredded mozzarella cheese

1. Preheat the grill on high.

2. Add half of the tomato slices, olives, cheese, and oregano to each side of the English muffin. About 2 minutes of broiling are required to melt the cheese.

NUTRITION FACTS (PER SERVING)

Calories: 213	Carbohydrates: 35g	Fat: 5g	Protein: 11g

24. Spinach, Peanut Butter & Banana Smoothie

Prep Time: 5 minutes

Serves: 1

Enjoying at least one of your recommended daily servings of leafy greens will be a sheer pleasure thanks to this delicious and sweet peanut butter, banana, and spinach smoothie. The traditional pairing of peanut butter and banana is made even tastier by the addition of tart, probiotic-rich kefir. Additionally, the addition of a little mild-flavored spinach to this peanut butter banana smoothie helps you increase your daily vegetable servings.

- 1 tablespoon peanut butter
- 1 cup plain kefir
- 1 cup spinach
- 1 tablespoon honey (optional)
- 1 frozen banana

1. In a blender, mix the kefir, peanut butter, spinach, banana, and honey (if using). Blend until smooth.

NUTRITION FACTS (PER SERVING)

Calories: 324	Carbohydrates: 45g	Fat: 11g	Protein: 16g

25. Egg Salad, Avocado Toast

Prep Time: 5 minutes

Serves: 1

This quick and healthy breakfast only takes five minutes to prepare.

- 1 tablespoon celery
- ¼ avocado
- ½ teaspoon lemon juice
- 1 slice whole-wheat toast
- Pinch of salt
- ½ teaspoon hot sauce
- 1 chopped hard-boiled egg

1. In a small bowl, mash avocado with celery, lemon juice, spicy sauce, and salt. Add the hard-boiled egg and mix. Spread on toast.

NUTRITION FACTS (PER SERVING)

Calories: 230	Carbohydrates: 17g	Fat: 14g	Protein: 11g

26. Quick-Cooking Oats

Prep Time: 5 minutes

Serves: 1

Basic is better sometimes. That is most often the case when eating breakfast. You can learn the basic techniques from these simple oatmeal recipes and consistently produce creamy, delicate oats. You can choose your own toppings and flavors.

- Pinch of salt
- 1 cup water or low-fat milk
- ½ cup quick-cooking oats (see tip)
- 1 to 2 teaspoons cane sugar, honey, or brown sugar for serving
- 1 oz low-fat milk for serving
- Pinch of cinnamon

1. On the stove, mix salt and water (or milk) in a small saucepan up to a boil. Oats are added once the heat is reduced to medium. Cook for 1 minute. Turn off the heat, cover the pan, and let it stand for two to three minutes.

2. For microwave: Salt, water (or milk), and oats should all be mixed in a 2-cup bowl that is microwave-safe. 1-2 minutes on High in the microwave. Stir before serving.

3. Serve with your preferred garnishes, such as milk, sugar, cinnamon, almonds, dried fruit, and sweetener.

NUTRITION FACTS (PER SERVING)

Calories: 150	Carbohydrates: 27g	Fat: 3g	Protein: 5g

27. Ricotta & Yogurt Parfait

Prep Time: 5 minutes

Serves: 1

This nutritious breakfast meal, which tastes like lemon cheesecake, is easy to put together in the morning. Alternately, mix the filling the night before and add the fruit, nuts, and seeds when you get to work.

- ¼ cup part-skim ricotta
- ¾ cup nonfat vanilla Greek yogurt
- ½ teaspoon lemon zest
- 1 tablespoon slivered almonds
- ¼ cup raspberries
- 1 teaspoon chia seeds

1. In a bowl, mix the yogurt, ricotta, and lemon zest. Add raspberries, almonds, and chia seeds as garnish.

NUTRITION FACTS (PER SERVING)

| Calories: 272 | Carbohydrates: 25g | Fat: 10g | Protein: 22g |

28. Southwest Breakfast Quesadilla

Prep Time: 5 minutes

Serves: 1

Beverage Paring: Tomato juice

This quick meal is tasty and filling, thanks to pico de gallo and cheesy eggs.

- ¼ cup refrigerated or frozen egg product, thawed
- Nonstick cooking spray, e.g., olive oil
- 1/8 to 1/4 teaspoon of salt-free southwest chipotle seasoning blend
- Chopped tomato plus more or 2 tablespoons refrigerated fresh pico de gallo for garnish
- 2 tablespoons shredded part-skim mozzarella cheese
- 1 whole-wheat flour tortilla
- 2 tablespoons of canned, no-salt-added black beans, rinsed and drained

1. Apply olive oil to a medium nonstick skillet. Heat a skillet to medium-low. Add one egg to a heated skillet and season with the spice mix. The egg should be cooked without stirring over medium heat, until it begins to set around the edges and on the bottom. Lift and fold the partially cooked egg with a spatula or large spoon so that the uncooked piece flows beneath. Cook the egg for a further 30 to 60 seconds over medium heat or until it is fully cooked but still glossy and moist.

2. Pour a cooked egg onto one side of the tortilla right away. Add cheese, beans, and 2 tablespoons of pico de gallo on top. Cover the filling with a folded tortilla and carefully press.

3. Use a paper towel to clean the same skillet. Apply frying spray to the skillet. Heat a skillet to medium-low. Cook the filled tortilla in a hot skillet for about 2 minutes, or until the filling is heated through and the tortilla is browned. Add more pico de gallo on top if desired.

NUTRITION FACTS (PER SERVING)

Calories: 175	Carbohydrates: 25g	Fat: 5g	Protein: 19g

29. Breakfast Salad with Egg & Salsa Verde Vinaigrette

Prep Time: 10 minutes   Serves: 1

A morning salad? Before you dismiss something, give it a shot. We adore the fact that this breakfast provides 3 whole cups of vegetables.

- 1 teaspoon and 1 tablespoon of extra-virgin olive oil, divided
- 3 tablespoons salsa verde, like Frontera brand
- 2 tablespoons chopped cilantro, plus more for toppings
- 8 blue corn tortilla chips, broken into big pieces
- 2 cups mesclun or any other salad greens
- ½ cup canned red kidney beans rinsed
- 1 large egg
- ¼ avocado, sliced

1. Salsa with 1 Tbsp. Cilantro and oil in a small bowl. Place half of the mixture in a shallow dinner bowl with the mesclun (or other greens).

2. Top the salad with a layer of chips, beans, and avocado.

3. Warm up the final one teaspoon of oil in a small skillet over medium-high heat. Add egg and cook for about two minutes, or until the white is fully cooked, but the yolk is still a little runny.

4. Serve the salad with the egg. Add more cilantro, if desired, and drizzle with the leftover salsa vinaigrette.

NUTRITION FACTS (PER SERVING)

Calories: 527	Carbohydrates: 37g	Fat: 34g	Protein: 16g

30. Peanut Butter & Chia Berry Jam English Muffin

Prep Time: 10 minutes

Serves: 1

This heart-healthy breakfast meal includes chia seeds in the quick "jam" topping, which increases the omega-3 fatty acids.

- 2 teaspoons of chia seeds
- 1 whole-wheat English muffin, toasted
- ½ cup unsweetened mixed frozen berries
- 2 teaspoons of natural peanut butter

1. Microwave the berries in a medium bowl (microwave-safe) for an additional 30 seconds after stirring. Add the chia seeds and stir.

2. On the English muffin, spread peanut butter. Add the berry-chia mixture on top.

NUTRITION FACTS (PER SERVING)

Calories: 262	Carbohydrates: 41g	Fat: 9g	Protein: 10g

LUNCH RECIPES

CHAPTER THREE

LUNCH RECIPES

You may have a variety of bothersome issues as a result of chronic inflammation, such as tight joints and poor digestion. In light of this, changing up your diet to include more nutrient-dense anti-inflammatory foods like cauliflower, avocado, and salmon can be a healthy way to do so. The staples of the Mediterranean diet, such as whole grains, fish, fruits, and vegetables, are included in these delectable meals that are suitable for the diet. You can flavor up your next midday meal with dishes like our Chopped Salad with Chickpeas, Olives & Feta, and Vegetarian Protein Bowl.

31. Chopped Salad with Chickpeas, Olives & Feta

Prep Time: 15 minutes

Serves: 4

Beverage Paring: Coconut water

Mediterranean flavors are what inspired the chickpeas, cucumber, and feta in this quick and easy chopped salad. A savory oil and vinegar dressing unites the ingredients.

- 2 tablespoons red-wine vinegar
- 2 tablespoons extra-virgin olive oil
- ¼ teaspoon garlic powder
- ¼ teaspoon ground pepper
- ¼ teaspoon salt
- 1 (15 ounces) can of no-salt-added chickpeas, rinsed
- 1 cup quartered cherry tomatoes
- 1 cup diced cucumber
- ⅓ cup chopped parsley
- ¼ cup halved Kalamata olives
- ¼ cup finely chopped red onion
- ¼ cup crumbled feta

1. In a big bowl, mix oil, vinegar, garlic powder, salt, and pepper. Toss in the chickpeas, feta, cucumber, tomatoes, parsley, onion, and olives.

NUTRITION FACTS (PER SERVING)

| Calories: 256 | Carbohydrates: 24g | Fat: 14g | Protein: 9g |

32. Cauliflower Rice Bowls with Grilled Chicken

Prep Time: 30 minutes

Serves: 4

Even though they only require 30 minutes to prepare, these delicious and healthful cauliflower rice bowls with feta, olives, vegetables, and grilled chicken are amazing.

- 4 cups of cauliflower rice
- 1 teaspoon and 6 tablespoons extra-virgin olive oil, divided
- ⅓ cup chopped red onion
- ½ cup chopped fresh dill, divided
- ¾ teaspoon salt, divided
- 1 pound of boneless, skinless chicken breasts
- 3 tablespoons lemon juice
- ½ teaspoon ground pepper, divided
- 1 teaspoon dried oregano
- 1 cup chopped cucumber
- 1 cup halved cherry tomatoes
- 2 tablespoons chopped Kalamata olives
- 4 wedges Lemon wedges for serving
- 2 tablespoons crumbled feta cheese

1. Preheat the grill to medium heat.

2. Warm two tablespoons of oil in a skillet over medium-high heat. Add 1/4 teaspoon salt, the onion, and the cauliflower. Cook for five minutes, stirring periodically, or until the cauliflower is tender. Add 1/4 cup dill and turn the heat off.

3. In the meantime, rub a teaspoon of oil all over the chicken. Add a quarter teaspoon each of pepper and salt. Grill for about 15 minutes total, flipping once or until an instant-read thermometer placed into the thickest portion of the breast registers 165 degrees F. Slice diagonally.

4. In another small bowl, combine the remaining 4 tablespoons of oil, oregano, lemon juice, and the last 1/4 teaspoon of salt and pepper.

5. The cauliflower rice should be divided into 4 dishes. Add the feta, tomatoes, cucumber, olives, and chicken on top. Add the final 1/4 cup of dill. Use the vinaigrette as a drizzle. If desired, garnish with lemon slices.

NUTRITION FACTS (PER SERVING)

Calories: 411	Carbohydrates: 10g	Fat: 28g	Protein: 29g

V vg

33. Baked Falafel Sandwiches

Prep Time: 40 minutes

Serves: 4

This falafel sandwich is thick, tart, and herbaceous in flavor. While the veggies inside make the falafel simple and fresh, the falafel bakes up lovely and crispy. To make preparation simple, prepare the tahini sauce in advance. Wrap it in foil to make the sandwich a portable lunch that stays intact while being consumed on the go.

- ½ cup chopped fresh flat-leaf parsley
- 1 (15 ounces) can of no-salt-added chickpeas, rinsed
- ½ cup chopped fresh cilantro
- ¼ cup panko breadcrumbs
- 1 cup thinly sliced, divided, and ½ cup grated red onion
- 1 tablespoon tahini
- 2 tablespoons lemon juice, divided
- 1 teaspoon grated lemon zest
- 1 teaspoon ground cumin
- 1 large clove of garlic, grated
- ¼ teaspoon salt
- 1 cup thinly sliced English cucumber
- 4 (10-inch) whole-wheat wraps
- 1 ½ tablespoons extra-virgin olive oil
- 2 cups of loosely packed arugula
- 1 recipe for Tahini Sauce with Garlic & Lemon
- 1 large tomato, cut into 8 slices

1. Set the oven to 350 degrees Fahrenheit (1760C). Cover the foil on a baking pan with extra-virgin oil.

2. In a food processor, combine the parsley, chickpeas, cilantro, chopped onion, panko, tahini, lemon zest, 1 tablespoon lemon juice, cumin, salt, and garlic. Process for 10 to 12 pulses, occasionally stopping to scrape down the sides until a coarse meal forms. Form the mixture into 4 patties that are each about 1/2 cup in size and 1/2 inch thick.

3. Put the patties on the baking sheet that has been prepared; spray the tops with extra-virgin oil. Bake for ten minutes. Flip the patties over, then spray extra-virgin oil on top. Continually bake for 10 to 12 more minutes or until golden brown.

4. In the meantime, mix the sliced onion, cucumber, oil, and the final tablespoon of lemon juice in a medium bowl. Allow to stand at room temperature for about 20 minutes while stirring occasionally.

5. Take the patties out of the oven and allow them to cool for five minutes. Slice in half.

6. Wraps should be placed directly on oven racks and baked for about a minute or until they are just warmed through.

7. Toss the arugula into the cucumber mixture to incorporate. On a work surface, arrange the warmed wraps. Top them evenly with the arugula mixture, half-falafels, tahini sauce, and tomato slices. Working with one wrap at a time, fold one edge of the wrap over the middle, then roll it up burrito-style. Wrap some foil around the bottom half to keep the wrap together.

NUTRITION FACTS (PER SERVING)

Calories: 517	Carbohydrates: 65g	Fat: 24g	Protein: 16g

34. Lentil Salad with Feta, Tomatoes, Cucumbers & Olives

Prep Time: 15 minutes

Serves: 6

To have on hand for a quick lunch, prepare this Mediterranean lentil salad with chopped vegetables, feta cheese, and a simple vinaigrette.

- 1-pint of multicolored cherry tomatoes, halved
- 3 cups of cooked brown lentils
- 1 ½ cups chopped English cucumber
- ½ cup thinly sliced red onion
- ½ cup coarsely chopped pitted Kalamata olives
- ½ cup crumbled feta cheese
- ½ teaspoon ground pepper, divided
- ½ teaspoon salt, divided
- ¼ cup extra-virgin olive oil
- 3 tablespoons red-wine vinegar
- ½ teaspoon minced garlic
- 1 tablespoon finely chopped shallot
- ½ teaspoon honey

1. In a big bowl, mix lentils, tomatoes, cucumber, olives, onion, feta, and 1/4 teaspoon each of salt and pepper.

2. In a small bowl, combine vinegar, honey, shallot, garlic, and the last 1/4 teaspoon of salt and pepper. Whisk in oil gradually until thoroughly mixed. Mix the lentil mixture with the dressing very gently. Serve right away or store in the fridge for up to five days.

NUTRITION FACTS (PER SERVING)

Calories: 271	Carbohydrates: 25g	Fat: 15g	Protein: 11g

35. Avocado Tuna Spinach Salad

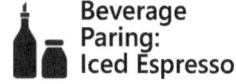

Prep Time: 10 minutes

Serves: 1

Beverage Paring: Iced Espresso

This protein-rich Avocado Tuna Salad with Spinach is ideal for a speedy, light lunch or dinner and will have you back in your summer clothes in no time. Avocado provides creaminess, and sunflower seeds offer structure and crunch in this simple tuna spinach salad.

- ¼ cup diced avocado
- ½ (5 ounces) can of water-packed tuna
- ¼ cup halved cherry tomatoes
- 1 tablespoon diced red onion
- 1 ½ tablespoons poppy seed dressing
- 1 tablespoon extra-virgin olive oil
- 1 tablespoon sunflower seeds
- 2 cups of baby spinach

1. In a medium bowl, mix the avocado, tuna, tomatoes, dressing, onion, and oil. Sprinkle sunflower seeds on top of the spinach before serving.

NUTRITION FACTS (PER SERVING)

Calories: 432	Carbohydrates: 17g	Fat: 32g	Protein: 20g

36. Mediterranean Quinoa Salad

Prep Time: 15 minutes

Serves: 6

REFRIGIRATE: OVERNIGHT

This quinoa and fresh vegetable salad from the Mediterranean region is marinated in a zesty, light vinaigrette. It's a simple vegetarian dinner recipe that can be prepared ahead of time for a nutritious lunch option.

- 6 tablespoons red-wine vinegar
- ½ cup extra-virgin olive oil
- 3 tablespoons chopped fresh oregano
- 1 ½ teaspoons Dijon mustard
- 1 ½ teaspoons honey
- ¼ teaspoon crushed red pepper
- 2 cups of thinly sliced English cucumber
- 3 cups cooked quinoa, cooled (see Associated Recipes)
- 1 ½ cups thinly sliced red onion
- ½ cup halved pitted Kalamata olives
- 1 cup halved grape tomatoes
- 1 (15 ounces) can of no-salt-added chickpeas, rinsed
- 3 cups of baby spinach (about 3 ounces)
- 1 cup crumbled feta, divided

1. In a big bowl, combine oil, vinegar, oregano, honey, Dijon, and crushed red pepper. Add quinoa, 1/2 cup feta, cucumber, onion, tomatoes, olives, and chickpeas. Gently blend by tossing. Cover and refrigerate for 30 minutes.

2. Spinach should be added and mixed carefully. Serve right away after adding the last 1/2 cup of feta.

NUTRITION FACTS (PER SERVING)

Calories: 472	Carbohydrates: 39g	Fat: 30g	Protein: 12g

37. Chickpea Tuna Salad

Prep Time: 20 minutes

Serves: 4

Beverage Paring: Fresh Grapefruit Juice

You can pack this chickpea tuna salad with cucumber, feta, capers, and olives for work or school. The salad can be prepared the night before; just remember to separate the spinach and season it just before serving.

- 1 tablespoon nonpareil capers, rinsed and chopped
- 2 tablespoons lemon juice
- 1 tablespoon finely chopped shallot
- ¼ teaspoon ground pepper
- ¼ teaspoon salt
- 1 (15 ounces) can of no-salt-added chickpeas, rinsed
- 1 cup halved cherry tomatoes
- 1 (6.7 ounces) jar oil-packed tuna, drained
- 3 cups of baby spinach
- 1 cup thinly sliced English cucumber
- 2 tablespoons chopped fresh dill
- ½ cup crumbled feta cheese
- 3 tablespoons extra-virgin olive oil

1. In a sizable bowl, combine the lemon juice, capers, shallot, salt, and pepper. Observe for five minutes.

2. In the meantime, combine the chickpeas, tuna, tomatoes, cucumber, feta, and dill in a large dish.

3. The lemon juice mixture and oil should be thoroughly combined. 5 tablespoons of the dressing should be poured over the chickpea mixture; toss to combine.

4. Toss the spinach with the remaining dressing in the big bowl. Four plates of spinach should be evenly distributed; add 1 1/4 cups of the chickpea mixture to each plate. Serve right away.

NUTRITION FACTS (PER SERVING)

Calories: 357	Carbohydrates: 23g	Fat: 19g	Protein: 21g

38. Salmon Rice Bowl

Prep Time: 10 minutes
Cook Time: 15 minutes
Serves: 2

This salmon rice bowl, which is inspired by the popular TikTok fad, is a delicious lunch or dinner option. You can prepare a wonderful meal in about 25 minutes using healthy foods like salmon, vegetables, and instant brown rice.

- 1 teaspoon avocado oil
- 4 ounces' salmon, preferably wild
- ⅛ teaspoon kosher salt
- 1 cup water
- 1 cup instant brown rice
- 2 tablespoons mayonnaise
- 1 ½ teaspoons of 50%-less-sodium tamari
- 1 ½ teaspoons Sriracha
- 1 teaspoon mirin
- ¼ teaspoon crushed red pepper
- ½ teaspoon freshly grated ginger
- ⅛ teaspoon kosher salt
- 12 (4-inch) sheets of nori (roasted seaweed)
- ½ cup chopped cucumber
- ½ ripe avocado, chopped
- ¼ cup spicy kimchi

1. Set the oven to 400°F. A small baking sheet with a rim should be foil-lined. Salmon should be put on the prepared pan. Add salt and drizzle with oil. Bake for 8 to 10 minutes or until an instant-read thermometer put in the thickest section reads 125°F.

2. In the meantime, mix the water and rice in a small saucepan and cook the rice as directed on the package. Combine mayonnaise and Sriracha in a small bowl; leave aside. In another little bowl, stir the tamari, mirin, ginger, crushed red pepper, and salt.

3. Distribute the rice between the two dishes. Add salmon, avocado, cucumber, and kimchi on top. Add a drizzle of the tamari and mayonnaise mixture. If desired, combine the bowls, then serve with nori.

NUTRITION FACTS (PER SERVING)

Calories: 481	Carbohydrates: 47g	Fat: 25g	Protein: 18g

39. Vegetarian Protein Bowl

Prep Time: 30 minutes

Cook Time: 30 minutes

Serves: 4

You can get everything you need for a complete meal in this vegetarian protein bowl. Beans give the farro mixture smoothness in addition to an increase in protein. The dish is brightened by chimichurri sauce.

- 1 ¼ cups farro
- 8 cups of water
- 1 (15-ounce) can of no-salt-added cannellini beans, rinsed
- 1 (1 pound) sweet potato, peeled and cut into 1-inch cubes
- 4 cups of cauliflower florets
- 2 tablespoons extra-virgin olive oil plus ¼ cup, divided
- ¾ teaspoon salt, divided
- 2 teaspoons lemon-pepper seasoning, divided
- 1 (6-ounce) bunch of fresh broccolini cut into 2-inch pieces
- ¼ cup chopped fresh cilantro
- ½ cup chopped fresh flat-leaf parsley
- 1 tablespoon red-wine vinegar
- ½ teaspoon crushed red pepper
- 1 large clove of garlic, grated
- ¼ cup chopped Castelvetrano olives

1. Set the oven to 425 °F (2180C). Use parchment paper to line a big baking sheet with a rim. Boil a pot of water. Stir in the farro. Return to a boil; lower heat to medium; and simmer at a low boil, uncovered, for about 30 minutes, or until the grains have swelled but are still al dente.

2. During the final 5 minutes of cooking, toss in the cannellini beans. Turn off the heat and drain. Cover to remain warm.

3. In the meantime, spread out the cauliflower florets and sweet potato on the prepared baking sheet. Add 1 1/2 tablespoons of oil, 1 1/2 teaspoons of lemon pepper, and 1/4 teaspoon of salt. Toss to combine, then distribute evenly on the pan.

4. In a medium bowl, mix broccolini, 1/2 tablespoon oil, and the final 1/2 teaspoon of lemon pepper; toss to coat. Roast the sweet potatoes and cauliflower for 20 minutes, or until almost soft. Remove from the oven, then push the cauliflower and sweet potatoes to one side. Add the broccolini to the opposite side of the pan and roast for 10 minutes, or until the vegetables are fork-tender and faintly browned.

5. Make the chimichurri by combining parsley, cilantro, vinegar, garlic, crushed red pepper, olives, and the remaining 1/4 cup oil with 1/2 teaspoon salt in a small bowl. Mix the farro mixture with 1/4 cup of the chimichurri.

6. Distribute the farro mixture among the four bowls, then top each one with an even layer of the roasted veggies and the final 1/4 cup of chimichurri.

NUTRITION FACTS (PER SERVING)

Calories: 572	Carbohydrates: 78g	Fat: 24g	Protein: 17g

40. Avocado Chicken Salad

Prep Time: 15 minutes

Serves: 6

Beverage Paring: Infused water (Cucumber and mint)

This is a creamy, vibrant, and herbaceous avocado chicken salad. Fresh avocado and the mixture of cilantro, dill, and chives go well together. Enjoy this simple chicken salad in a wrap, on lettuce, or over crackers.

- ½ cup coarsely chopped fresh chives and more for garnish
- ½ cup of tightly packed fresh cilantro leaves and tender stems
- ¼ cup tightly packed fresh dill fronds
- 1 teaspoon of lemon zest and more for garnish
- 1 tablespoon of drained capers
- 1 tablespoon lemon juice
- ¾ teaspoon salt
- 2 cloves of garlic
- ½ teaspoon ground pepper
- 3 cups shredded cooked chicken breast
- ⅓ cup mayonnaise
- 2 ripe avocados, halved and pitted, divided
- ¼ cup whole-milk plain strained yogurt (such as Greek style)

1. In a food processor, mix the avocado flesh, cilantro, chives, dill, capers, lemon zest, lemon juice, garlic salt, and pepper. Process until the mixture is finely minced, about 30 seconds. Add yogurt and mayonnaise; process for 1 to 2 minutes or until smooth.

2. Chop up the remaining avocado and put it in a bowl. Add the chicken and the dressing, and gently mix until everything is incorporated and coated. Serve at room temperature or put it in the fridge for two hours to get it cold. If preferred, add more chives and lemon zest as a garnish.

NUTRITION FACTS (PER SERVING)

Calories: 321	Carbohydrates: 7g	Fat: 22g	Protein: 24g

41. Vegetarian Chopped Power Salad and Creamy Cilantro Dressing

Prep Time: 25 minutes

Serves: 4

Chickpeas and quinoa are added to this nutritious vegetarian salad recipe to improve the protein content. When combined to create a creamy dressing, cilantro adds color and flavor. Serve this chilled salad for lunch or dinner.

- ¼ cup buttermilk
- ½ cup chopped cilantro
- ¼ cup mayonnaise
- 1 tablespoon cider vinegar
- 2 tablespoons chopped shallot
- ¼ teaspoon salt
- 6 cups of torn lettuce
- ¼ teaspoon ground pepper
- 2 cups finely sliced, stemmed kale
- 2 medium carrots, sliced
- 1 (15 ounces) can chickpeas, rinsed
- 1 diced medium yellow or red bell pepper
- ⅓ cup roasted unsalted pepitas
- 1 cup cooked quinoa

1. In a small food processor, mix the cilantro, buttermilk, mayonnaise, shallot, vinegar, salt, and pepper. Blend thoroughly after processing.

2. In a big bowl, mix quinoa, lettuce, kale, chickpeas, carrots, and bell pepper. Drizzle the dressing and give it a good toss to coat the salad. Pepitas should be added just before serving.

NUTRITION FACTS (PER SERVING)

Calories: 362	Carbohydrates: 38g	Fat: 17g	Protein: 13g

42. Avocado Tuna Salad

Prep Time: 15 minutes

Serves: 6

Beverage Paring: Rooibos tea

REFRIGIRATE: OVERNIGHT

This simple avocado tuna salad dish will liven up a tuna can. Smooth avocado offers creaminess, which is balanced out by feta cheese's saline flavor and a squeeze of lemon's acidity. Cucumber and romaine hearts provide a cooling crunch.

- 2 tablespoons lemon juice
- 3 tablespoons extra-virgin olive oil
- ¼ teaspoon salt
- 2 (5 ounces) cans of solid white tuna in oil, drained and flaked
- 2 medium avocados, chopped (about 2 ½ cups)
- 4 cups of romaine hearts
- ⅓ cup crumbled feta cheese
- 1 cup chopped English cucumber
- ¼ cup toasted sliced almonds
- 3 tablespoons chopped fresh flat-leaf parsley
- ¼ cup chopped pitted Kalamata olives

1. In a big bowl, whisk together the lemon juice, oil, and salt. Add the avocados and gently toss to coat. Toss the tuna, romaine, cucumber, feta, nuts, olives, and parsley gently into the avocado mixture. Serve right away or refrigerate for up to an hour.

NUTRITION FACTS (PER SERVING)

Calories: 338	Carbohydrates: 10g	Fat: 27g	Protein: 17g

43. Winter Greens Bowl

Prep Time: 20 minutes

Serves: 4

There are still vegetables in season, even though it is winter. Brassica family members, which include vegetables like the broccoli and cauliflower used in this recipe and leafy greens like the arugula in the pesto, are cheerful and sweet throughout the cooler months. The green color of pumpkin seeds is an homage to the winter squash kept in cool, dark places like the pantry. The result is the Winter Green Bowls, a celebration of the flora that surrounds us and is evergreen regardless of the time of year.

Greens Bowl

- 1 cup low-sodium vegetable broth
- 1 medium head of cauliflower, cut into florets
- ½ cup quinoa
- ½ cup chopped walnuts, toasted
- 4 cups chopped kale
- ¼ teaspoon salt
- 1 (15-ounce) can of no-salt-added cannellini beans, rinsed

Dressing

- 3 tablespoons water
- ¾ cup whole-milk plain Greek yogurt
- 1 tablespoon extra-virgin olive oil
- 2 teaspoons of cider vinegar
- ¼ teaspoon ground pepper
- 1 clove of garlic, minced
- 1 teaspoon lemon zest
- ½ teaspoon ground turmeric
- 2 tablespoons lemon juice
- ¼ teaspoon salt

1. To prep the greens bowl, fill a big saucepan with 1 inch of water, then fit a steamer basket within. Over high heat, add the cauliflower and bring to a boil. About 5 minutes of covered steaming will yield tender results. Cauliflower should be moved to a big bowl and covered to maintain warmth. Throw away the water.

2. Fill the pan with stock, quinoa, and salt. Bring to a boil. Cook for five minutes, then reduce the heat to low. Add the beans and kale after stirring, and cook for 5 to 8 minutes or until the quinoa has absorbed all the liquid. Add cauliflower, cover, and turn off the heat.

3. To prep the dressing: In a separate bowl, stir together the yogurt, water, oil, garlic, vinegar, lemon zest, lemon juice, turmeric, pepper, and salt.

4. Pour the dressing on the quinoa mixture and top with the walnuts.

NUTRITION FACTS (PER SERVING)

Calories: 381	Carbohydrates: 41g	Fat: 18g	Protein: 18g

44. Quinoa-Black Bean Salad

Prep Time: 20 minutes

Serves: 6

Use this quinoa and black bean salad as a filling side dish for grilled chicken or steak or as a quick and tasty vegetarian main dish. Not to forget the leftovers! On the go, they are a simple lunch option.

- 1 medium zucchini, cut lengthwise into 1/4-inch planks
- 2 ears of corn, husks removed
- 6 tablespoons extra-virgin olive oil
- 1 ½ teaspoons ground cumin
- ¼ cup lime juice
- 3 cups cooked quinoa (see Associated Recipes)
- 1 (15-ounce) can of no-salt-added black beans, rinsed
- 3 cups of baby arugula
- 1 cup pico de gallo, divided
- ¾ cup crumbled cotija cheese, divided
- ½ cup chopped fresh cilantro, divided
- 1 avocado, diced, divided

1. Heat a gas grill or charcoal to medium (350–400 degrees Fahrenheit or 2040C). For about 10 minutes, grill corn with the lid off and sometimes turn it until it is soft and browned all over. Uncovered, for 2 minutes on each side, grill zucchini until browned and tender. (An alternative would be to cook the food in a grill pan that has been sprayed with extra-virgin oil. Grill corn for 4 to 5 minutes, turning regularly, until browned and soft. Grill zucchini for about 2 minutes on each side, flipping once, until browned and tender.) Cut the corn kernels off the cobs and coarsely slice the zucchini.

2. In a sizable bowl, combine the oil, lime juice, and cumin. Add half of the pico de gallo, cilantro, cheese, avocado, quinoa, beans, corn, zucchini, and corn. Gently blend by tossing.

3. Add the remaining avocado, cheese, cilantro, and pico de gallo over the top.

NUTRITION FACTS (PER SERVING)

Calories: 458	Carbohydrates: 47g	Fat: 26g	Protein: 14g

45. White Bean Veggie Salad

Prep Time: 10 minutes

Serves: 1

White beans and avocado are combined in this tasty, meatless main dish salad. Try experimenting with various seasonal vegetables.

For this salad, we used diced cucumbers and cherry tomatoes, but you are welcome to substitute any other veggies you want or have on hand, such as bell peppers, radishes, or celery. Try experimenting with various seasonal vegetables. Ensure that any leftover roasted veggies are totally cool before incorporating them into the salad.

- ¾ cup veggies of your choice, such as cherry tomatoes and chopped cucumbers
- 2 cups of mixed salad greens
- ⅓ cup canned white beans rinsed and drained
- 1 tablespoon red-wine vinegar
- ½ avocado, diced
- 2 teaspoons extra-virgin olive oil
- Freshly ground pepper to taste
- ¼ teaspoon kosher salt

1. In a medium bowl, combine the greens, veggies, beans, and avocado. Add pepper and salt, and drizzle with vinegar and oil.

2. Transfer to a large platter after tossing to blend.

NUTRITION FACTS (PER SERVING)

Calories: 360	Carbohydrates: 30g	Fat: 25g	Protein: 10g

46. Tomato, Cucumber & White-Bean Salad with Basil Vinaigrette

Prep Time: 25 minutes

Serves: 4

Use the sweetest cherry or grape tomatoes and juicy cucumbers of the season in this no-cook bean salad for a light meal or lunch. An easy vinaigrette recipe transforms a plain salad into something amazing by adding fresh basil.

- ¼ cup extra-virgin olive oil
- ½ cup packed fresh basil leaves
- 3 tablespoons red wine vinegar
- 2 teaspoons Dijon mustard
- 1 tablespoon finely chopped shallot
- 1 teaspoon honey
- ¼ teaspoon ground pepper
- ¼ teaspoon salt
- 10 cups of mixed salad greens
- 1 cup halved cherry or grape tomatoes
- 1 (15 ounces) can of low-sodium cannellini beans, rinsed
- ½ cucumber halved lengthwise and sliced (1 cup)

1. In a small food processor, mix the oil, basil, vinegar, shallot, mustard, honey, salt, and pepper. Process till it's largely seamless. Place it in a large bowl. Add greens, beans, tomatoes, and cucumber. Coat by tossing.

NUTRITION FACTS (PER SERVING)

Calories: 246	Carbohydrates: 22g	Fat: 15g	Protein: 8g

47. Mediterranean Chickpea Quinoa Bowl

Prep Time: 20 minutes

Serves: 4

Beverage Paring: Apricot nectar

REFRIGIRATE: OVERNIGHT

This grain bowl for vegetarians is loaded with plant-based protein from quinoa and chickpeas. Make a large batch of these tasty grain bowls and store them in covered containers in the refrigerator for quick, wholesome grab-and-go lunches all week.

- ¼ cup slivered almonds
- 1 (7 ounces) jar of roasted red peppers, rinsed
- 4 tablespoons extra-virgin olive oil, divided
- 1 teaspoon paprika
- 1 small clove of garlic, minced
- ½ teaspoon ground cumin
- 2 cups of cooked quinoa
- ¼ teaspoon crushed red pepper (optional)
- ¼ cup Kalamata olives, chopped
- 1 (15 ounces) can chickpeas, rinsed
- ¼ cup finely chopped red onion
- 1 cup diced cucumber
- 2 tablespoons finely chopped fresh parsley
- ¼ cup crumbled feta cheese

1. In a small food processor, combine the peppers, almonds, 2 tablespoons oil, garlic, paprika, cumin, and crushed red pepper (if using). Puree until largely smooth.

2. In a medium bowl, mix the quinoa, olives, red onion, and the last 2 tablespoons of oil.

3. To assemble each bowl, add equal portions of the chickpeas, cucumber, and red pepper sauce to the quinoa mixture. Add some feta and parsley.

NUTRITION FACTS (PER SERVING)

| Calories: 479 | Carbohydrates: 50g | Fat: 25g | Protein: 13g |

V gf vg

48. Vegan Grain Bowl

Prep Time: 30 minutes

Serves: 4

Sweet potatoes, protein-packed chickpeas, creamy avocado, and homemade tahini dressing are just a few of the delicious ingredients in this simple grain bowl. Prepare the whole recipe over the weekend and store it in individual serving containers for weeklong work lunches that are ready to go.

- 3 tablespoons extra-virgin olive oil, divided
- 1 medium sweet potato, sliced into 1-inch chunks, peeled if you like
- ½ teaspoon salt, divided
- 2 tablespoons tahini
- ½ teaspoon ground pepper, divided
- 2 tablespoons water
- 1 small clove of garlic, minced
- 1 tablespoon lemon juice
- 2 cups of cooked quinoa
- 1 firm, ripe avocado, diced
- 1 15-ounce can of chickpeas, rinsed
- ¼ cup chopped fresh cilantro or parsley

1. Set the oven to 425 Fahrenheit (2180C).

2. In a larger bowl, combine the sweet potato with 1/4 teaspoon of salt, 1 tablespoon of oil, and 1/4 teaspoon of pepper. Move it to a baking sheet with a rim. Cook for 15 to 18 minutes, stirring once, until fork-tender.

3. Prepare a small bowl by mixing the remaining 2 tablespoons of oil, the tahini, the water, the lemon juice, the garlic, and the last 1/4 teaspoon of salt and pepper.

4. To assemble, divide the quinoa among the four bowls. Add equal portions of avocado, chickpeas, and sweet potatoes on top. Add a drizzle of tahini sauce. Add some cilantro or parsley.

NUTRITION FACTS (PER SERVING)

Calories: 455	Carbohydrates: 51g	Fat: 25g	Protein: 11g

V vg

49. Couscous & Chickpea Salad

Prep Time: 5 minutes

Serves: 1

Beverage Paring: Iced lemon balm tea

This simple lunch salad combines cooked couscous and canned chickpeas. This salad tastes everything but basic, thanks to the basil vinaigrette! When fresh tomatoes are in season, we suggest adding them to tabbouleh to give them a new flavor.

- ¾ cup cooked whole-wheat couscous
- 4 tablespoons Basil Vinaigrette
- 1 cup finely chopped kale
- ⅔ cup rinsed canned chickpeas

1. In a medium bowl, combine the couscous, chickpeas, kale, and dressing. Serve right away or store in the fridge for up to 4 days in a container that can be sealed.

NUTRITION FACTS (PER SERVING)

Calories: 481	Carbohydrates: 68g	Fat: 17g	Protein: 17g

V gf vg

50. Quinoa Chickpea Salad and Roasted Red Pepper Hummus Dressing

Prep Time: 10 minutes

Serves: 1

This robust vegan salad is made up of a variety of plant-based superfoods, including chickpeas, quinoa, and hummus. We enjoy the sunflower seeds' crunch and the unexpected flavor of the roasted peppers.

- 1 tablespoon lemon juice
- 2 tablespoons hummus, roasted or original red pepper flavor
- 1 tablespoon chopped roasted red pepper
- ½ cup cooked quinoa
- 2 cups of mixed salad greens
- ½ cup chickpeas, rinsed
- Pinch of ground pepper
- 1 tablespoon chopped fresh parsley
- 1 tablespoon unsalted sunflower seeds
- Pinch of salt

1. In a bowl, mix the lemon juice, hummus, and red peppers. Thin with water to the desired dressing consistency.

2. In a big bowl, combine the greens, quinoa, and chickpeas. Add parsley, sunflower seeds, salt, and pepper on top. Serve with the dressing.

NUTRITION FACTS (PER SERVING)

Calories: 379	Carbohydrates: 59g	Fat: 11g	Protein: 16g

51. Tomato-&-Avocado Cheese Sandwich

Prep Time: 15 minutes

Serves: 1

My tomato and avocado grilled cheese sandwich, which takes a simple sandwich idea and makes it taste somewhat more gourmet with the addition of avocado and tomato, is ready in about 15 minutes. Your palate will appreciate it!
Because parmesan cheese has such a strong flavor, only 1/4 cup is required to give this vegetarian toaster oven sandwich a powerful flavor boost. Get some fruit as well when you pair the sandwich with a juicy pear.

- ¼ avocado, mashed
- 2 slices of whole-wheat bread
- 3 slices of tomato
- 1 cup of mixed salad greens or baby spinach
- 1 medium-ripe pear
- ¼ cup grated Parmesan cheese
- 2 teaspoons balsamic vinegar

1. Place the bread on the work surface. Spread avocado on one slice. Add cheese and tomatoes on top. In a toaster oven, toast both pieces of bread for 4 to 6 minutes, or until the topped piece has melted cheese and the plain piece is toasted.

2. Collect the toast from the toaster oven and pile spinach or greens on top of the cheese side using a spatula. Add vinegar, then add the remaining toast on top. If preferred, slice in half and serve with pear.

NUTRITION FACTS (PER SERVING)

| Calories: 439 | Carbohydrates: 63g | Fat: 15g | Protein: 18g |

52. Meal-Prep Falafel Bowls

Prep Time: 20 minutes

Serves: 4

Beverage Paring: Carrot and ginger juice

⊙ REFRIGIRATE: OVERNIGHT

Thanks to healthful convenience foods like frozen falafel and fresh green beans that are steamed in a bag, these quick couscous bowls can be prepared in just 20 minutes. Mix the simple tahini sauce while the other components cook.

- ⅔ cup water
- 1 (8-ounce) package of frozen prepared falafel
- ½ cup whole-wheat couscous
- ¼ cup crumbled feta cheese
- 1/2 cup Tahini Sauce (see associated recipe)
- 1 (16-ounce) bag of steam-in-bag fresh green beans
- ¼ cup pitted Kalamata olives

1. Prepare falafel as directed on the package, then leave it aside to cool.

2. In a little pan, bring water to a boil. Add the couscous, cover it, and turn off the heat. Allow to stand for approximately 5 minutes, or until the liquid is absorbed. Use a fork to fluff, then set aside.

3. Prepare the green beans as directed on the box.

4. Assemble the tahini sauce. Distribute among 4 small lidded condiment containers before refrigerating.

5. Distribute the green beans among 4 individuals, lidded containers. Each should have 1 tablespoon of feta, 1 tablespoon of olives, and 1/4 cup of falafel on top. Seal and store in the fridge for up to 4 days.

6. Reheat in the microwave for two minutes or until well-cooked before serving. Dress with tahini sauce just prior to eating.

NUTRITION FACTS (PER SERVING)

Calories: 500	Carbohydrates: 55g	Fat: 27g	Protein: 15g

53. Chicken & Apple Kale Wraps

Prep Time: 10 minutes

Serves: 1

This low-calorie (and lower-carbohydrate) healthy chicken lunch recipe uses kale leaves rather than bread to wrap your meal. Try cabbage for your wrap if you can't get lacinato (also known as Tuscan) kale.

- 1 teaspoon Dijon mustard
- 1 tablespoon mayonnaise
- 3 medium lacinato kale leaves
- 6 thin red onion slices
- 3 ounces of thinly sliced cooked chicken breast
- 1 firm apple, cut into 9 slices

1.In a small bowl, mix mustard and mayo. Apply it to the kale leaves. Each leaf should have 1 ounce of chicken, 2 onion slices, and 3 apple slices on top. Each leaf should be wrapped. If desired, divide it in half.

NUTRITION FACTS (PER SERVING)

Calories: 370	Carbohydrates: 34g	Fat: 14g	Protein: 29g

54. Veggie & Hummus Sandwich

Prep Time: 10 minutes

Serves: 1

Beverage Paring: Chia Seed Smoothie

This mile-high sandwich with hummus and vegetables is the ideal vegetarian meal on the go. Mix it up with several hummus varieties and different vegetables, depending on how you're feeling.

- 3 tablespoons hummus
- 2 slices of whole-grain bread
- ¼ avocado, mashed
- ¼ cup shredded carrot
- ¼ medium red bell pepper sliced
- ½ cup mixed salad greens
- ¼ cup sliced cucumber

1. On one slice of bread, spread hummus; on the other, avocado. Add greens, bell pepper, cucumber, and carrot to the sandwich. Cut in half, then present.

NUTRITION FACTS (PER SERVING)

Calories: 325	Carbohydrates: 40g	Fat: 14g	Protein: 13g

55. Orzo Salad with Chickpeas & Artichoke Hearts

Prep Time: 30 minutes

Serves: 2

You'll want to prepare a sizable quantity of this Mediterranean orzo salad to store in the refrigerator as cookouts and picnics in the warm weather are again on the agenda. It's ideal to bring to an unplanned neighborhood gathering and is fantastic to take for a quick and healthy lunch at the beach.

- 1 ½ teaspoons extra-virgin olive oil
- 1/2 cup of orzo or other tiny pasta
- 1 clove of garlic, crushed and peeled
- 1 ½ tablespoons lemon juice
- ⅛ teaspoon salt
- ⅛ teaspoon freshly ground pepper
- 1 7-ounce can of chickpeas, rinsed
- 1 drained and chopped 14-ounce can of artichoke hearts
- 2 cups of baby spinach leaves
- ⅓ cup crumbled feta cheese
- 1 ½ tablespoons chopped fresh mint
- 2 tablespoons chopped fresh dill
- 1 large tomato, chopped

1. Boil water in a small pan. Cook 0rzo as directed on the package or for about 9 minutes or until just tender. Drain and coolly rinse with cold water. Press to get rid of the extra water. Toss with oil in a medium bowl after transfer.

2. Mash salt and garlic into a paste in a medium bowl with the back of a spoon. Add pepper and lemon juice by whisking. Stir gently to mix the cooked orzo, artichokes, chickpeas, feta, dill, and mint. Re-toss after adding tomatoes.

3. Distribute the spinach and then the salad on two plates.

NUTRITION FACTS (PER SERVING)

Calories: 436	Carbohydrates: 73g	Fat: 8g	Protein: 19g

56. Black Bean-Quinoa Bowl

Prep Time: 10 minutes

Serves: 1

This black bean and quinoa bowl would be more like a taco salad if it didn't have a fried bowl. In addition to a simple hummus dressing, the dish also includes pico de gallo, fresh cilantro, and avocado.

- ⅔ cup cooked quinoa
- ¾ cup canned black beans rinsed
- 2 tablespoons chopped fresh cilantro
- ¼ cup hummus
- ¼ medium avocado, diced
- 1 tablespoon lime juice
- 3 tablespoons pico de gallo

1. Combine the quinoa and beans in a bowl. Hummus and lime juice should be combined in a small bowl; add water too thin to the desired consistency. Over the quinoa and beans, drizzle the hummus dressing. Top with cilantro, avocado, and pico de gallo.

NUTRITION FACTS (PER SERVING)

Calories: 500	Carbohydrates: 74g	Fat: 16g	Protein: 20g

57. Salmon-Stuffed Avocados

Prep Time: 15 minutes

Serves: 4

A useful pantry essential and convenient way to add heart-healthy, omega-3-rich seafood to your diet is canned salmon. In this dish, we pair it with avocados for a simple, no-cook meal.

- ½ cup diced celery
- ½ cup nonfat plain Greek yogurt
- 2 tablespoons chopped fresh parsley
- 2 teaspoons mayonnaise
- 1 tablespoon lime juice
- 1 teaspoon Dijon mustard
- ⅛ teaspoon ground pepper
- ⅛ teaspoon salt
- 2 (5 ounces) cans of salmon, drained, flaked, bones, and skin removed
- Chopped chives for garnish
- 2 avocados

1. In a medium bowl, mix the celery, yogurt, parsley, mayonnaise, lime juice, mustard, salt, and pepper. Stir in the fish well.

2. Pit avocados and cut them in half lengthwise. Remove about 1 tablespoon of flesh from each avocado half and put it in a small bowl. Mash the avocado flesh that has been removed and combine it with the salmon mixture with a fork.

3. Place a heap of the salmon mixture, equal to 1/4 cup of each avocado half, on top of each avocado half. If desired, add chives as a garnish.

NUTRITION FACTS (PER SERVING)

Calories: 293	Carbohydrates: 11g	Fat: 20g	Protein: 23g

58. Kale & Quinoa Salad with Lemon Dressing

Prep Time: 25 minutes

Serves: 6

This kale-quinoa salad is bursting with various tastes and textures. The kale's fibrous texture can be broken down by massaging it, while toppings like feta, cucumber, and toasted walnuts provide crunch and saltiness.

- 6 tablespoons extra-virgin olive oil
- 1 bunch of lacinato kale, stemmed and chopped
- 3 tablespoons lemon juice
- 1 teaspoon of honey
- 2 tablespoons chopped shallot
- ½ teaspoon salt
- 2 cups of grape or cherry tomatoes, halved
- ¼ teaspoon ground pepper
- 2 cups cooked quinoa
- 1 medium red bell pepper, sliced
- 1 English cucumber, thinly sliced
- 1 medium yellow bell pepper, sliced
- ¾ cup feta cheese, crumbled
- 1 (15-ounce) can of unsalted chickpeas, rinsed
- ½ cup sliced almonds, toasted

1. Fill a big serving bowl with greens. In a small bowl, stir together the oil, lemon juice, shallot, honey, salt, and pepper. Pour two to three tablespoons of the dressing over the kale and lightly massage for 1 to 2 minutes, or until the kale begins to wilt.

2. Add tomatoes, quinoa, cucumber, peppers, chickpeas, feta, and almonds to the kale as a topping. Sprinkle with the remaining dressing and toss before serving.

NUTRITION FACTS (PER SERVING)

| Calories: 400 | Carbohydrates: 37g | Fat: 23g | Protein: 14g |

gf

59. Pesto Chicken Quinoa Bowls

Prep Time: 15 minutes

Cook Time: 45 minutes

Serves: 6

Beverage Paring: Sparkling Pomegranate Water

This pesto chicken quinoa bowl is loaded with an Italian spice blend and basil pesto herbs, and the red pepper adds just a touch of heat. This recipe can also be made with orzo in place of quinoa if you like the flavor profile.

- 3 cloves of garlic, minced
- 1 tablespoon dried Italian seasoning
- 1 ¼ teaspoons salt
- ½ teaspoon crushed red pepper
- ¾ teaspoon ground pepper
- 1 ½ pounds of boneless, skinless chicken thighs
- 2 cups of cherry tomatoes
- 2 medium zucchini, cut into half-inch-thick half-moons
- 1 ¾ cups water
- 2 tablespoons extra-virgin olive oil
- 1 cup of white quinoa
- Thinly sliced fresh basil for garnish
- ½ cup prepared basil pesto

1. Set the oven to 400oF. Wrap foil around a sizable baking sheet with a rim. In a bowl, mix the Italian seasoning, garlic, salt, pepper, and crushed red pepper.

2. In a bowl, combine the zucchini, chicken, tomatoes, oil, and Italian spice blend. Stir to mix. On the baking sheet that has been prepared, arrange the chicken and veggies in a single layer.

3. About 20 minutes into roasting, check that the tomatoes are beginning to burst, the zucchini is fork-tender, and the instant-read thermometer placed into the thickest part of the chicken indicates 165°F. Remove from oven; let stand for ten minutes to cool. Use two forks to shred the chicken after transferring it to a platter.

4. Quinoa and water should be mixed in a medium saucepan and heated to a rolling boil. Reduce heat to low, cover, and simmer for 12 to 15 minutes or until liquid is absorbed. Withdraw from the heat and let it stand for five minutes. Fluff with a fork.

5. In a sizable bowl, add the cooked quinoa and the roasted vegetables, along with any accumulated liquids from the baking sheet. Add the pesto and carefully mix everything together until smooth. Put the mixture in six bowls. Chicken shreds should be distributed equally on top; basil may be added as a garnish.

NUTRITION FACTS (PER SERVING)

Calories: 327	Carbohydrates: 15g	Fat: 21g	Protein: 23g

60. Kale & Avocado Salad with Blueberries & Edamame

Prep Time: 20 minutes

Serves: 4

This California-inspired salad is a delightful and filling way to get your vitamins and is bursting with nutrient-rich fruit. We adore the unusual combination of goat cheese, edamame, and blueberries.

- 1 avocado, diced
- 6 cups stemmed and coarsely chopped curly kale
- 1 cup of blueberries
- 1 cup cooked, shelled edamame
- 1 cup halved yellow cherry tomatoes
- ¼ cup sliced almonds, toasted (see Tip)
- ¼ cup olive oil
- ½ cup crumbled goat cheese (2 ounces)
- 1 teaspoon of salt
- 3 tablespoons lemon juice
- 1 ½ teaspoons honey
- 1 tablespoon minced chives
- 1 teaspoon Dijon mustard

1. Place the kale in a big bowl and knead the leaves with your hands to make them softer. Add goat cheese, edamame, tomatoes, avocado, and blueberries.

2. In a small bowl or jar with a secure lid, mix the oil, lemon juice, chives, honey, mustard, and salt. Strongly whirl or shake.

3. Pour the vinaigrette over the salad and mix well.

NUTRITION FACTS (PER SERVING)

Calories: 368	Carbohydrates: 21g	Fat: 29g	Protein: 10g

SNACK RECIPES

CHAPTER FOUR

SNACK RECIPES

These packable snack recipes are delicious and nutritious solutions to avoid mid-afternoon hunger. These dishes make it easy to adhere to the Mediterranean diet because they are balanced with whole grains, legumes, fruits, and vegetables. The Mediterranean diet is among the healthiest eating regimens to adhere to, and because it is flexible, it may be easier for you to maintain over time. Make these snacks in advance to grab-and-go on hectic days. Recipes like our Fig & Honey Yogurt and Rosemary-Garlic Pecans make filling snacks in between meals.

61. Rosemary-Garlic Pecans

Prep Time: 5 minutes

Cook Time: 1 hour, 15 minutes

Serves: 12

Beverage Paring: Lemon water

These savory spiced nuts are ideal for a cheese board, a snack, or a small appetizer. These rosemary-garlic pecans are excellent as a snack or as an addition to your entertaining platters. They are dairy-, gluten-, and vegan-free. A little bit salty, a little bit sweet, flavorful, and dangerously good! Pecans from Barefoot Farm are a great choice for vegetarian and meat-free diets because they are high in protein and antioxidants.

- 3 tablespoons dried rosemary, finely chopped
- 3 cups of pecans
- 1 large egg white
- 2 teaspoons of garlic salt

1. Set the oven to 250°F (1210C).

2. In a larger bowl, combine the garlic salt, rosemary, and egg white. Pecans should be added and coated. Spread out in a uniform layer on a sizable baking sheet with a rim.

3. Bake for around 45 minutes, stirring every 15 minutes, until dry. Allow it to cool completely for around 30 minutes before storing.

NUTRITION FACTS (PER SERVING)

Calories: 175	Carbohydrates: 4g	Fat: 18g	Protein: 3g

62. Homemade Trail Mix

Cook Time: 5 minutes

Serves: 5

Trail mix varieties vary widely. With the help of this lesson on how to make a healthy trail mix, you'll discover the insider secrets what to include and exclude, as well as how to customize your own trail mix to your needs and preferences! Try this with a portable mix that contains any combination of nuts and dried fruits.

- ¼ cup unsalted dry-roasted peanuts
- ¼ cup whole shelled (unpeeled) almonds
- ¼ cup dried cranberries
- Peanut butter
- 2 ounces of dried apricots, or other fruit
- ¼ cup chopped pitted dates

1. In a medium bowl, mix dates, apricots (or other fruit), cranberries, almonds, peanuts, and peanut butter.

NUTRITION FACTS (PER SERVING)

| Calories: 132 | Carbohydrates: 15g | Fat: 7g | Protein: 4g |

63. Savory Date & Pistachio Bites

Prep Time: 10 minutes

Serves: 32

Beverage Paring: Green tea

These bite-sized treats are ideal as an on-the-go snack or as a complement to a cheese board because they have a hint of sweetness from the dates and raisins and crunch and nuttiness from the pistachios.

- 1 cup raw unsalted shelled pistachios
- 2 cups pitted whole dates
- 1 cup of golden raisins
- ¼ teaspoon ground pepper
- 1 teaspoon ground fennel seeds

1. In a food processor, combine dates, pistachios, raisins, fennel, and pepper. Process until very finely chopped. Make approximately 32 balls using one tablespoon each.

NUTRITION FACTS (PER SERVING)

| Calories: 68 | Carbohydrates: 13g | Fat: 2g | Protein: 1g |

vg

64. Lime & Parmesan Popcorn

Cook Time: 10 minutes

Serves: 1

Make your own flavored popcorn to satisfy your hunger for a snack instead of buying a bag of microwaved popcorn. Parmesan cheese, lime zest, and a touch of chile powder are used in this healthy popcorn recipe, but feel free to substitute your preferred seasonings. Use olive oil cooking spray to help the toppings adhere to the popcorn for the finest flavor.

- Olive oil cooking spray
- 2 cups plain air-popped popcorn
- 1 tablespoon Parmesan cheese
- Pinch of chili powder
- 1 teaspoon lime zest
- Pinch of salt

1. Sprinkle popcorn with salt, Parmesan, chili powder, lime zest, and a light coating of cooking spray.

NUTRITION FACTS (PER SERVING)

Calories: 113	Carbohydrates: 14g	Fat: 5g	Protein: 4g

65. Fig & Honey Yogurt

Cook
Time:
5 minutes

Serves:
1

The fig and honey yogurt bowl is a wonderfully quick and simple meal for breakfast or a snack. Protein-rich, making achieving your protein goal easy. You must try this yogurt dish if you're seeking a low-fat, high-protein meal that will keep you full and leave you feeling content and happy. Dried figs and honey are sprinkled on plain yogurt in this snack with a Mediterranean flavor. Use fresh figs as a substitute if you can locate them.

- 3 dried figs, sliced
- ⅔ cup low-fat plain yogurt
- 2 teaspoons of honey

1. Put yogurt in a bowl with figs and honey on top.

NUTRITION FACTS (PER SERVING)

| Calories: 208 | Carbohydrates: 39g | Fat: 3g | Protein: 9g |

66. Apricot-Sunflower Granola Bars

Prep Time: 20 minutes

Cook Time: 1 hour 10 minutes

Serves: 1

Beverage Paring: Herbal Infusions such as mint or chamomile tea

These nut-free granola bars are easy to make at home and may be customized to your liking. Simply adjust the additions to your preferences by substituting 2 cups of any two of the dried fruit, seeds, or chocolate chips listed below for the apricots and seeds in this version. We experimented with various gooey sweeteners, such as honey and maple syrup, but discovered that brown rice syrup held the bars together the best.

- 1 cup crispy brown rice cereal
- 3 cups old-fashioned rolled oats
- 1 cup of nicely-chopped dried apricots (1/4 inch)
- ½ cup of unsalted pepitas toasted
- ¼ teaspoon salt
- ½ cup unsalted sunflower seeds toasted
- ½ cup sunflower seed butter
- ⅔ cup of light corn syrup or brown rice syrup
- 1 teaspoon of ground cinnamon

1. Turn the oven's temperature up to 325 degrees (1620C). In a 9 by 13-inch baking pan, line the edges and the bottom with parchment paper, leaving some of it dangling over the sides. Apply some olive oil to the parchment paper lightly.

2. In a sizable bowl, mix the oats, rice cereal, pepitas, sunflower seeds, and salt.

3. In a bowl that can be heated in the microwave, mix rice syrup (or corn syrup), sunflower butter, and cinnamon. Thirty seconds in the microwave (or 1 minute in a saucepan over medium heat). The addition and dry components should be mixed to combine. When transferring, press firmly into the pan with the back of a spatula.

4. To make chewier bars, bake for 25 minutes, or until the edges are just starting to darken but the center is still soft. For crunchier bars, bake for 35 minutes, or until the edges are golden brown and the centers are still somewhat gooey. (Both remain soft when warm and become firmer as they cool.)

5. For easier lifting out of the pan onto a chopping board (it will still be soft), let it cool in the pan for ten minutes. Slice into 24 bars, then refrigerate for a further 30 minutes without separating the bars. Cut into bars after cooling.

NUTRITION FACTS (PER SERVING)

Calories: 152	Carbohydrates: 22g	Fat: 6g	Protein: 4g

67. Carrot Cake Energy Bites

Prep Time: 15 minutes

Serves: 22

The good news is that producing those protein balls from carrot cake couldn't be easier. Additionally, this recipe for vegan protein balls doesn't call for vegan protein powder. In actuality, there are a variety of nuts and seeds from which you can obtain vegan proteins. So, allow me to demonstrate my secret for making inexpensive vegan protein balls with dates. These no-cook energy bites are easy to grab on the move and store well in the fridge or freezer.

- ½ cup old-fashioned rolled oats
- 1 cup pitted dates
- ¼ cup chopped pecans
- 2 medium carrots (about 4 oz. total), finely chopped
- ¼ cup chia seeds
- 1 teaspoon of vanilla extract
- ½ teaspoon ground ginger
- ¾ teaspoon ground cinnamon
- ¼ teaspoon ground turmeric
- Pinch of ground pepper
- ¼ teaspoon salt

1. In a food processor, mix the dates, oats, pecans, and chia seeds; pulse several times to blend and chop.

2. When the paste starts to form, add the carrots, vanilla, cinnamon, ginger, turmeric, salt, and pepper. Process until all the ingredients are finely minced.

3. Make little 1 Tbsp-sized balls out of the mixture.

NUTRITION FACTS (PER SERVING)

Calories: 48	Carbohydrates: 8g	Fat: 2g	Protein: 1g

68. Everything-Seasoned Almonds

Prep Time: 5 minutes

Cook Time: 1 hour 20 minutes

Serves: 12

The everything bagel seasoning will stick to the almonds better if it is ground up in a spice grinder. These Everything Seasoned Almonds are the ideal healthy nut snack because everyone loves them! A little salty, savory, oniony, garlicky, and sesame seed-studded for even more texture. They are addictive, so use caution!

- 3 tablespoons everything bagel seasoning, ground
- 1 large egg white
- 3 cups raw, unsalted almonds

1. Set the oven to 250°F (1210C).

2. In a medium bowl, mix the spice and egg white. Add almonds and toss to coat. On a large baking sheet with a rim, spread it out in a uniform layer.

3. Bake for around 45 minutes, stirring every 15 minutes, until dry. Allow it to cool completely for around 30 minutes before storing.

NUTRITION FACTS (PER SERVING)

Calories: 223	Carbohydrates: 8g	Fat: 18g	Protein: 8g

69. Date-Pistachio Granola Bars

Prep Time: 20 minutes

Cook Time: 1 hour, 10 minutes

Serves: 1

Beverage Paring: Almond milk latte

These homemade granola bars have components that are often found in Middle Eastern cuisine, including dates, hazelnuts, pistachios, tahini, and cardamom. However, feel free to change the nuts, seeds, dried fruit, and/or spices to your liking. We tried a bunch of goopy sweeteners, such as maple syrup and honey, but found out that brown rice syrup held the bars together the best.

- 1 cup crispy brown rice cereal
- 3 cups old-fashioned rolled oats
- 1 cup of nicely chopped pitted dates, preferably Medjool (1/4 inch)
- ½ cup unsalted pistachios, toasted and chopped
- ½ cup hazelnuts, toasted and chopped
- ¼ teaspoon salt
- ½ cup tahini
- ⅔ cup of brown rice syrup or light corn syrup
- 1 teaspoon ground cardamom

1. Turn the oven's temperature up to 325 degrees (1620C). A 9 by 13-inch baking pan should be lined with parchment paper, leaving part of it dangling over the sides. On the parchment paper, lightly apply cooking spray.

2. In a sizable bowl, mix the oats, rice cereal, dates, hazelnuts, pistachios, and salt.

3. In a pan that can withstand the microwave, mix the cardamom, tahini, and rice syrup (or corn syrup). Thirty seconds in the microwave (or 1 minute in a saucepan over medium heat). The addition and dry components should be mixed to combine. When transferring, press firmly into the pan with the back of a spatula.

4. To make chewier bars, bake for 25 minutes, or until the edges are just starting to darken but the center is still soft. For crunchier bars, bake for 30 to 35 minutes, or until the edges are golden brown and the centers are still somewhat gooey. (Both remain soft when warm and become firmer as they cool.)

5. For easier lifting out of the pan onto a chopping board (it will still be soft), let cool in the pan for ten minutes. Slice into 24 bars, then refrigerate for a further 30 minutes without separating the bars. Cut into bars after cooling.

NUTRITION FACTS (PER SERVING)

| Calories: 155 | Carbohydrates: 23g | Fat: 6g | Protein: 3g |

(V) (gf) (vg)

70. Seneca White Corn No-Bake Energy Balls

Prep Time: 15 minutes **Serves:** 36

This recipe, which Kaylena Bray gave us, came from her parents David and Wendy Bray. They both teach Seneca White Corn in New York State and impart their expertise at practical courses held by colleges, Native community centers, and farms all across the nation. The combination of oats and maize flour, peanut butter, coconut, dried fruit, and mixed nuts gives these no-bake energy balls a lot of staying power. By varying the dried fruit and nuts, they are easily adaptable.

- 1 cup of roasted white corn flour
- 1 ½ cups quick oats
- 1 teaspoon of ground cinnamon
- ½ cup natural peanut butter
- 1 teaspoon of salt
- ¼ cup unsweetened applesauce
- 2 tablespoons water
- 2 tablespoons pure maple syrup
- 2 tablespoons honey
- ½ cup of unsalted roasted mixed chopped nuts, such as walnuts, almonds, pecans, and/or hazelnuts
- ½ cup of unsweetened coconut flakes and more for rolling
- 1 teaspoon of vanilla extract
- ½ cup of dried fruit, such as currants and/or raisins

1. Line a baking sheet with parchment paper.

2. In a medium bowl, mix the oats, corn flour, cinnamon, and salt. Add the peanut butter, applesauce, maple syrup, honey, vanilla, and 2 tablespoons of water. Add the coconut flakes, almonds, and dried fruit and gently whisk.

3. Roll the mixture into 1-inch balls with clean hands, using about 1 heaping spoonful for each. Roll in additional coconut, if desired (if the mixture is too dry to roll, whisk with 1 tablespoon of water).

NUTRITION FACTS (PER SERVING)

Calories: 77	Carbohydrates: 9g	Fat: 4g	Protein: 2g

71. Kale Chips

Prep Time: 25 minutes

Cook Time: 10 minutes

Serves: 4

Beverage Paring: Sparkling water with citrus

Don't you like kale? These crunchy baked kale chips will win you over! Avoid packing the baking pans too tightly for the best outcome. Any variety of kale can be made into a kale chip, from curly kale's ruffled leaves to the dark ridges of lacinato. Our only recommendation is to choose organic kale if at all possible. Nonorganic food may have significant pesticide residues that are difficult to wash off entirely.

- 1 tablespoon extra-virgin olive oil
- 1 large bunch of kale, leaves torn into pieces (about 16 cups), tough stems removed
- ¼ teaspoon salt

1. Place the oven's racks in the upper third and the center, and warm it to 400°F (2040C).

2. Transfer the kale to a big bowl after completely patting any moisture off with a clean dish towel. Drizzle salt and oil over the kale. Use your hands to knead the kale leaves to evenly spread the salt and oil. Be careful to evenly distribute the kale leaves on 2 big rimmed baking pans. Make the chips in batches if all of the kale will not fit.

3. Bake for about ten minutes, rotating the pans from top to bottom and back to front halfway through, or until the majority of the leaves are crisp. (If using just one baking sheet, check after 8 minutes to avoid scorching.)

NUTRITION FACTS (PER SERVING)

Calories: 110	Carbohydrates: 16g	Fat: 5g	Protein: 5g

72. Tuna Salad Spread

Prep Time: 5 minutes

Serves: 4

In place of mayonnaise, this tuna spread dish substitutes Greek yogurt and avocado for a healthier version of tuna salad. Serve it with whole-grain crackers, cucumber slices, or butter lettuce leaves.

- 2 tablespoons low-fat plain Greek yogurt
- 1 avocado, mashed
- 1 tablespoon of lemon juice
- ¼ teaspoon garlic powder
- 1 tablespoon chopped fresh parsley
- ¼ teaspoon paprika
- ¼ teaspoon ground pepper
- ¼ cup diced onion or celery
- ¼ teaspoon salt
- 1 (5 ounces) can of albacore tuna in water, drained

1. In a small dish, whisk together the avocado and yogurt.

2. Stir in the parsley, garlic powder, paprika, salt, and pepper after adding the lemon juice. Mix gently after adding the tuna and onion (or celery).

NUTRITION FACTS (PER SERVING)

Calories: 130	Carbohydrates: 6g	Fat: 8g	Protein: 10g

73. Curried Cashews

Prep Time: 5 minutes

Cook Time: 45 minutes

Serves: 48

Every time we produced these curry cashews, they were gone in an instant due to their extreme addictiveness. Leave out the extra salt if you're using salted cashews.

- 6 tablespoons curry powder
- 6 cups unsalted cashews
- 6 tablespoons lemon juice
- 4 teaspoons of kosher salt

1. Set oven racks in the upper and lower thirds and preheat to 250 degrees Fahrenheit (1210C).

2. In a big bowl, stir together salt, lemon juice, and curry powder. Add cashews and coat. Spread evenly on 2 large rimmed baking pans.

3. Bake for around 45 minutes, stirring every 15 minutes, until dry. Allow it to cool completely. Use an airtight container for storage.

NUTRITION FACTS (PER SERVING)

Calories: 101	Carbohydrates: 6g	Fat: 8g	Protein: 3g

74. Grilled Flatbread with Burrata Cheese

Prep Time: 15 minutes

Serves: 6

Burrata is a delicious summer delicacy that pairs well with charred grilled flatbread, luscious cherry tomatoes, and burrata.

- 4 metal or bamboo skewers soaked in water for 30 minutes
- 8 ounces of cherry tomatoes
- ½ cup of extra-virgin olive oil
- Freshly cracked black pepper
- Kosher salt
- 2 tablespoons chopped fresh basil
- 1-pound of fresh pizza dough
- 4 ounces Parmesan cheese, grated
- Flour for dusting
- 8 ounces of burrata, drained and torn

1. Turn the grill to medium heat.

2. Evenly distribute the tomatoes along the skewers. The skewers should be put on a big plate. Salt and pepper the tomatoes after brushing them with olive oil. To cook the skewers until they are soft and charred, place them on the grill and leave them there for 5 minutes before turning them over. Go back to the plate.

3. In the meantime, separate the dough into 4 equal sections. Roll each portion into 14-inch-thick rounds on a surface that has been lightly dusted with flour. Apply olive oil with a pastry brush to the dough's tops.

4. Brush the tops of the dough carefully with the remaining olive oil and place it on the grill, oil side down. Cook for about 5 minutes or until big bubbles start to appear on the surface. After flipping the dough, evenly distribute the Parmesan. Add the burrata evenly on top, and simmer uncovered for an additional 4-5 minutes or until the cheese starts to melt.

5. Placing the flatbread on a dish, adding basil and olive oil, and serving. Tomato skewers should be served alongside.

NUTRITION FACTS (PER SERVING)

Calories: 114	Carbohydrates: 34g	Fat: 57g	Protein: 23g

(V) (gf) (vg)

75. Easy Hummus

Prep Time: 10 minutes

Serves: 6

Beverage Paring: Coconut water

Making your own hummus is far simpler than buying it from the shop, and it tastes a lot better. Tahini is a sesame seed paste that we can create at home or omit if we don't have any on hand. Without it, a chickpea purée is still fairly tasty. Just increase the olive oil. This goes fantastically with flatbread.

- 1 large lemon
- 1/4 cup of lemon juice
- 1 ½ cups (250 grams) cooked chickpeas or 1 (15-ounce) can chickpeas
- 1/4 cup (60 ml) well-stirred tahini
- 2 tbsp of extra-virgin olive oil
- 1 small garlic clove, minced
- 1/2 teaspoon ground cumin
- 2 to 3 tablespoons (30 to 45 ml) water or aquafaba
- Salt to taste
- Dash with ground paprika or sumac for serving.

1. Place the lemon juice and tahini in the bowl of a food processor and process for 1 minute. After scraping down the bottom and sides of the bowl, process for an extra 30 seconds. This additional time is used to "whip" or "cream" the tahini, resulting in smooth and creamy hummus.

2. Mix the whipped tahini and lemon juice with the olive oil, cumin, minced garlic, and 1/2 teaspoon salt; after scraping the bowl's bottom and sides, process for a further 30 seconds or until everything is thoroughly mixed. Open, rinse, and drain the chickpeas. Fill the food processor with half the chickpeas. Take one minute to process. The remaining chickpeas should be added to the bowl after cleaning the sides and bottom and processed for one to two minutes or until thick and extremely smooth.

3. The hummus will probably be overly thick or contain little chickpea pieces. If this happens, fix it by gradually adding 2 to 3 tablespoons of water while the food processor is running until the appropriate consistency is reached.

4. After tasting, adjust the salt as necessary. Olive oil and paprika should be drizzled over the hummus before serving. Homemade hummus should be kept in the refrigerator for up to a week in an airtight container.

NUTRITION FACTS (PER SERVING)

Calories: 190	Carbohydrates: 18g	Fat: 11g	Protein: 6g

DINNER RECIPES

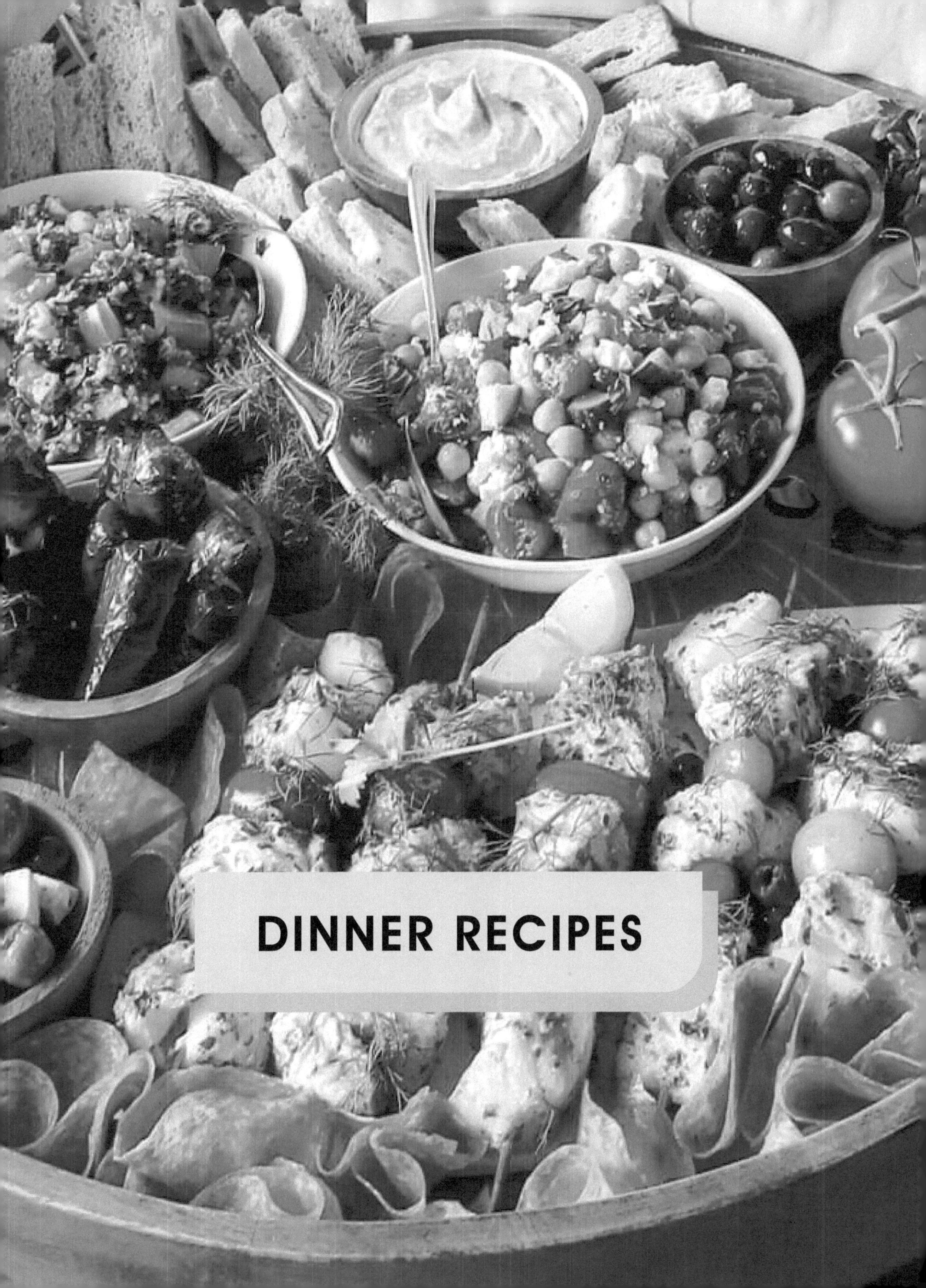

CHAPTER FIVE

DINNER RECIPES

The Mediterranean diet is among the healthiest eating habits in the world, which is rich in fruits, olive oil, vegetables, whole grains, and legumes. Here are some of our favorite dinner recipes for the Mediterranean diet, ranging from veggie-packed pasta to vibrant sheet-pan dishes.

76. Slow-Cooker Mediterranean Quinoa with Arugula

Prep Time: 15 minutes

Serves: 6

Packed with quinoa, chickpeas, and veggies, this salad can be a meal in and of itself. This Mediterranean diet meal gains texture and taste from the feta, lemon, olives, and roasted red peppers. For dinner, you may either serve the quinoa warm as a salad or cold. After boiling the quinoa, let it cool fully before serving.

- 1 ½ cups uncooked quinoa, rinsed
- 2 ¼ cups unsalted vegetable stock
- 1 cup of sliced red onions (from 1 onion)
- 1 (15.5 ounces) can of no-salt-added chickpeas (garbanzo beans), drained and rinsed
- 2 garlic cloves, minced (about 2 teaspoons)
- 2 ½ tablespoons olive oil
- 2 teaspoons of fresh lemon juice (from one lemon)
- ¾ teaspoon kosher salt
- 2 tablespoons coarsely chopped fresh oregano
- ½ cup of drained, chopped roasted red bell peppers (from a jar)
- 2 ounces of crumbled feta cheese (about 1/2 cup)
- 4 cups baby arugula (about 4 ounces)
- 12 pitted kalamata olives, halved lengthwise

1. In a slow cooker, mix the quinoa, stock, onions, chickpeas, garlic, 1/2 tablespoon olive oil, and 1/2 teaspoon salt. For 3 to 4 hours, with the lid on, simmer the quinoa on LOW until it is soft and the stock has been absorbed.

2. Turn off the slow cooker. With a fork, fluff the quinoa mixture. Mix the lemon juice, the remaining 1/4 tsp salt, and 2 tablespoons of olive oil in a bowl. Red bell peppers and the olive oil combination should be added to the slow cooker and gently mixed together.

3. Fold the arugula in slowly. Cover and leave out for about 10 minutes, or until the arugula is just beginning to wilt. The oregano, feta cheese, and olives should be distributed evenly over each serving.

NUTRITION FACTS (PER SERVING)

Calories: 352	Carbohydrates: 46g	Fat: 13g	Protein: 12g

77. Portobello Mushroom Pizzas Arugula Salad

Prep Time: 35 minutes

Cook Time: 10 minutes

Serves: 4

Roasted portobello mushrooms serve as the crust in these cozy little "pizzas." An easy side salad of arugula serves as a colorful complement.

- 2 tablespoons of olive oil plus 1 tsp., divided
- 8 large portobello mushroom caps (around 4 oz. each), gills removed
- ½ teaspoon ground pepper, divided
- 2 cups lightly packed baby spinach, chopped
- ½ cup pizza or tomato sauce
- ½ cup sun-dried tomatoes (about 8), chopped
- ½ cup shredded part-skim mozzarella cheese
- 1 (14-ounce) can of artichoke hearts, rinsed and chopped
- ¼ cup fresh basil leaves, thinly sliced
- ¼ cup crumbled feta cheese
- 1 tablespoon of lemon juice
- ½ teaspoon dried Italian seasoning
- 2 cups of lightly packed baby arugula

1. Turn on the oven to 400F (40C). Place a wire rack on a sizable baking sheet that has been lined with foil. Place portobello caps on the rack with their undersides facing up after brushing them with 1 tablespoon of oil. Roat for ten minutes. Flip and roast for five additional minutes.

2. After taking the portobellos out of the oven, carefully turn them over so that the undersides are now facing up. Pepper the food with 1/4 teaspoon. Each cap should have 1 Tbsp of sauce inside. Distribute the artichokes, feta, mozzarella, sun-dried tomatoes, and spinach among the caps. Add some Italian seasoning. Put the portobellos back into the oven and bake for an additional 10 to 15 minutes, or until the cheese is melted and beginning to brown.

3. In the meantime, mix the lemon juice remaining 1/8 tsp. Pepper, and 1 Tbsp. + 1 tsp. of oil in a medium bowl. Add and coat the arugula.

4. Add basil to the top of the portobello pizzas and serve them with the arugula salad.

NUTRITION FACTS (PER SERVING)

Calories: 264	Carbohydrates: 25g	Fat: 13g	Protein: 14g

78. Walnut-Rosemary Salmon

Prep Time: 10 minutes

Cook Time: 12 minutes

Serves: 4

Beverage Paring: Fresh Grapefruit Juice

Omega-3 fatty acids are rich in walnuts and salmon. For dinner, serve this quick dish of salmon with a walnut crust along with a simple salad and a side of roasted potatoes. To make this dish gluten-free, just swap out the panko breadcrumbs for gluten-free versions.

- 1 clove of garlic, minced
- 2 teaspoons Dijon mustard
- ¼ teaspoon lemon zest
- 1 teaspoon chopped fresh rosemary
- 1 teaspoon of lemon juice
- ½ teaspoon honey
- ¼ teaspoon crushed red pepper
- ½ teaspoon kosher salt
- 3 tablespoons panko breadcrumbs
- 1 teaspoon extra-virgin olive oil
- 3 tablespoons finely chopped walnuts
- 1 (1 pound) skinless salmon fillet, frozen or fresh
- Chopped fresh lemon wedges and parsley for garnish
- Olive oil cooking spray

1. Set the oven to 425 Fahrenheit (2180C). Use parchment paper to line a big baking sheet with a rim.

2. In a bowl, mix the garlic, mustard, lemon zest, rosemary, lemon juice, honey, salt, and red pepper flakes. In a different small bowl, mix the panko, walnuts, and oil.

3. Line the salmon on the lined baking sheet. After applying the mustard mixture to the fish, sprinkle the panko mixture over it and press firmly to help it stick. Apply cooking spray sparingly.

4. Depending on thickness, bake the fish for 8 to 12 minutes, or until it flakes effortlessly with a fork.

5. Top with parsley and, if preferred, serve with lemon wedges.

NUTRITION FACTS (PER SERVING)

Calories: 222	Carbohydrates: 4g	Fat: 12g	Protein: 24g

79. Cheesy Spinach-&-Artichoke Stuffed Spaghetti Squash

Prep Time: 25 minutes

Serves: 4

By substituting spaghetti squash for pasta, this delectable, creamy casserole has 75% fewer calories and carbohydrates. If you have enough time, roasting the squash is better than cooking it in the microwave since the flavor is sweeter and more intense.

- 3 tablespoons water divided
- 1 spaghetti squash, seeds removed; cut in half lengthwise.
- 1 (5-ounce) package of baby spinach
- 4 ounces of less-fat cream cheese, cubed and softened
- 1 (10-ounce) frozen artichoke hearts, thawed and chopped
- ½ cup grated Parmesan cheese, divided
- ¼ teaspoon ground pepper
- ¼ teaspoon salt
- Chopped fresh basil and crushed red pepper for garnish

1. Put the squash cut-side down in a dish that can be used in the microwave. Add 2 tablespoons of water. 10 to 15 minutes on High, uncovered, until tender. (Alternatively, set the cut-side-down squash halves on a rimmed baking sheet. Bake for around 40 to 50 minutes at 400°F (2040F) until tender.)

2. In the meantime, in a big skillet over medium heat, combine the spinach and the remaining 1 tablespoon of water. Cook for three to five minutes, stirring occasionally, until wilted. Transfer to a big bowl after draining.

3. Place the rack in the upper third of the oven and heat the broiler.

4. Scrape the squash from the shells into the bowl using a fork. Arrange the shells on a baking sheet. Add salt, pepper, 1/4 cup Parmesan, cream cheese, and artichoke hearts to the squash mixture. Add the remaining 1/4 cup of Parmesan on top after dividing it among the squash shells. For about 3 minutes, broil (cook) the cheese until it turns golden brown. If preferred, top with basil and red pepper flakes.

NUTRITION FACTS (PER SERVING)

Calories: 223	Carbohydrates: 23g	Fat: 11g	Protein: 10g

80. Feta & Roasted Red Pepper Stuffed Chicken Breasts

Prep Time: 25 minutes

Cook Time: 25 minutes

Serves: 8

Beverage Paring: Rooibos tea

Feta cheese, roasted peppers, spinach, and other ingredients found in the Mediterranean region served as inspiration for this quick and easy filled chicken breast recipe. The chicken is given a gorgeous golden color and cooked uniformly throughout in this healthy baked chicken recipe by browning it in a skillet before baking.

- ½ cup chopped roasted red bell peppers
- ½ cup crumbled feta cheese
- ½ cup chopped fresh spinach
- 1 tablespoon chopped fresh basil
- ¼ cup Kalamata olives, pitted and quartered
- 1 tablespoon chopped fresh flat-leaf parsley
- 4 (8-ounce) boneless, skinless chicken breasts
- 2 cloves garlic, minced
- ¼ teaspoon salt
- 1 tablespoon extra-virgin olive oil
- ½ teaspoon ground pepper
- 1 tablespoon of lemon juice

1. Set the oven to 4000F (2040C). In a medium bowl, combine the feta, spinach, olives, basil, parsley, and garlic.

2. To create a pocket, make a horizontal slit through the hardest part of each chicken breast using a tiny knife. Fill each breast pocket with about 1/3 cup of the feta mixture, and then use wooden picks to keep the pockets closed. Salt and pepper should be uniformly distributed on the chicken.

3. In a sizable oven-safe skillet, heat the oil over medium-high heat. Place the stuffed breasts in the pan with the tops facing down and cook for 2 minutes or until golden. Flip the chicken carefully, then place the pan in the oven. Bake for 20 to 25 minutes or until an instant-read thermometer injected into the thickest part of the chicken reads 165°F (730C). Lemon juice should be applied evenly to the chicken. Remove the wooden picks from the chicken before serving.

NUTRITION FACTS (PER SERVING)

Calories: 179	Carbohydrates: 2g	Fat: 7g	Protein: 24g

81. Skillet Chicken with Orzo & Tomatoes

Prep Time: 35 minutes

Serves: 4

In this nutritious chicken recipe, orzo that is just right al dente is served alongside chicken thighs that have been marinated in lemon, garlic, and herbs. This simple one-skillet entrée is made completely with charred tomatoes and onions.

- ¼ cup of fresh lemon juice
- 4 (6 ounces) bone-in, skin-on chicken thighs
- 3 cloves garlic, minced
- 2 teaspoons of nicely-chopped fresh oregano
- 1 tablespoon chopped fresh rosemary
- ½ teaspoon crushed fennel seeds
- ½ teaspoon salt
- 3 tablespoons extra-virgin olive oil, divided
- ½ teaspoon ground pepper
- 1-pint cherry tomatoes
- 1 large red onion, sliced (¼-inch)
- 1 cup uncooked orzo
- 1 ½ cups unsalted chicken broth
- ⅓ cup pitted Kalamata olives
- Chopped fresh flat-leaf parsley for garnish

1. In a sizable zip-top plastic bag, combine the lemon juice, chicken, garlic, oregano, fennel seeds, rosemary, and 2 tablespoons of oil. Refrigerate for 25 to 30 minutes after sealing the bag.

2. Drain the chicken after removing it from the marinade, then discard the marinade. Salt and pepper should be uniformly distributed on the chicken. Heat the last tbs of oil over medium-high heat in a 10-inch cast-iron pan. Place the chicken in the pan, skin-side down and cook for about 7 minutes, stirring occasionally, until browned and crispy. About 4 minutes after flipping, grill the opposite side until browned. Place on a platter. (The chicken won't be fully done.) Do not clean the pan.

3. Add the onion and tomatoes to the saucepan; simmer for about 5 minutes, turning regularly, until the tomatoes are blistered and the onion is charred.

4. Center the rack in the oven and preheat it to broil (cook). Stir in the orzo and the olives to the mixture in the skillet. Mix in the broth. Heat to a rolling boil over medium-high. Put the chicken in the mixture skin-side up and lower the heat to medium-low. Cover and simmer for 14 to 15 minutes untill the orzo is al dente and a thermometer placed into the thickest part of the chicken reads 165°F (730C).

5. Put away from heat and let stand for 5 minutes with a lid. Remove the cover and broil (cook) for 2 to 3 minutes or until the chicken skin is crisp. If preferred, add some parsley, oregano, and lemon juice as a garnish. Serve right away.

NUTRITION FACTS (PER SERVING)

Calories: 641	Carbohydrates: 44g	Fat: 37g	Protein: 32g

82. Charred Shrimp, Pesto & Quinoa Bowls

Prep Time: 25 minutes

Serves: 4

It takes less than 30 minutes to prepare these shrimp, pesto, and quinoa bowls, which are also delicious, healthful, and attractive. In other words, they're the ultimate easy weeknight dinner. You are welcome to add more veggies and substitute chicken, beef, tofu, or edamame for the shrimp.

- 2 tablespoons balsamic vinegar
- ⅓ cup prepared pesto
- 1 tablespoon extra-virgin olive oil
- ¼ teaspoon ground pepper
- ½ teaspoon salt
- 1-pound large shrimp (16-20 counts), peeled, deveined, and patted dry
- 1 avocado, diced
- 2 cups cooked quinoa
- 4 cups arugula
- 1 cup halved cherry tomatoes

1. In a big bowl, combine pesto, vinegar, oil, salt, and pepper. In each bowl, take 4 tablespoons of the mixture, and place them both aside.

2. A big cast-iron skillet should be heated at medium-high. Add the shrimp and stir-fry for 4 to 5 minutes or until just cooked through with a little char. Take it out onto a platter.

3. Toss the quinoa and arugula with the vinaigrette in a sizable bowl. The arugula mixture should be divided into 4 dishes. Add tomatoes, avocado, and shrimp on top. 1 tablespoon of the reserved pesto mixture should be drizzled over each bowl.

NUTRITION FACTS (PER SERVING)

| Calories: 429 | Carbohydrates: 29g | Fat: 22g | Protein: 31g |

83. Sheet-Pan Salmon with Sweet Potatoes & Broccoli

Prep Time: 30 minutes **Cook Time:** 15 minutes **Serves:** 4

This salmon sheet pan dinner has a ton of flavor thanks to the vibrant combination of cheese, cilantro, chile, and lime that takes its cue from Mexican street corn.

- 1 teaspoon chili powder
- 3 tablespoons low-fat mayonnaise
- 2 medium sweet potatoes, sliced and peeled into 1-inch cubes
- ½ teaspoon salt, divided
- 4 teaspoons olive oil, divided
- ¼ teaspoon ground pepper, divided
- 1 ¼ pounds of salmon fillet, cut into 4 portions
- 4 cups of broccoli florets (8 oz.; 1 medium crown)
- 2 limes, 1 juiced and zested, and 1 cut into wedges for serving
- ½ cup chopped fresh cilantro
- ¼ cup crumbled feta or cotija cheese

1. Set the oven to 425 degrees Fahrenheit (2180C). A sizable rimmed baking sheet should be lined with foil and sprayed with cooking spray.

2. In a small bowl, mix the mayonnaise and chili powder. Place aside.

3. Toss sweet potatoes with 1/4 tsp. salt, 2 tsp. oil, and 1/8 tsp. pepper in a medium bowl.

4. Spread out on the baking sheet you've prepared. Roast for 15 minutes.

5. Meanwhile, combine the remaining 2 tsp. oil, 1/8 teaspoon pepper, and 1/4 teaspoon salt with the broccoli in the same bowl.

6. Take the baking sheet out of the oven. The sweet potatoes should be stirred and moved to the pan's edges. Spread the broccoli between the sweet potatoes on either side of the salmon in the center of the pan.

7. Apply 2 Tbsp of the salmon to the mayonnaise mixture.

8. Bake for about 15 minutes, or until the salmon flakes effortlessly with a fork and the sweet potatoes are soft.

9. Add the remaining 1 Tbsp of lime juice and zest in the meantime. Mix the mayonnaise thoroughly.

10. Divide the salmon among the four dishes on top of the cheese and cilantro.

11. Distribute the broccoli and sweet potatoes among the plates, then top with the lime-mayonnaise sauce. Lime wedges and any leftover sauce should be served.

NUTRITION FACTS (PER SERVING)

Calories: 504	Carbohydrates: 34g	Fat: 26g	Protein: 34g

84. Slow-Cooker Mediterranean Diet Stew

Prep Time: 15 minutes

Serves: 6

This stew can be prepared in a slow cooker and is ideal for individuals following the Mediterranean diet because it focuses on veggies, fiber-rich legumes, and healthy fats. Try substituting collards or spinach for the kale, or change the chickpeas for white beans for a different flavor profile. The flavors of this simple vegan crockpot stew are brought together by a drizzle of olive oil.

- 3 cups low-sodium vegetable broth
- 2 (14-ounce) cans of no-salt-added fire-roasted diced tomatoes
- 1 cup coarsely chopped onion
- 4 cloves garlic, minced
- 1 bunch of lacinato kale, chopped and stemmed (about 8 cups)
- ¾ cup chopped carrot
- 1 teaspoon dried oregano
- ½ teaspoon crushed red pepper
- ¾ teaspoon salt
- ¼ teaspoon ground pepper
- 1 (15-ounce) can no-salt-added chickpeas, rinsed, divided
- 1 tablespoon lemon juice
- Fresh basil leaves, torn if large
- 3 tablespoons extra-virgin olive oil
- 6 lemon wedges (Optional)

1. In a 4-quart slow cooker, mix the tomatoes, broth, onion, carrot, garlic, oregano, salt, crushed red pepper, and pepper. Cook on Low for 6 hours with the cover on.

2. Pour 1/4 cup of the slow cooker's cooking liquid into a bowl. Add 2 tablespoons of chickpeas, then blend with a fork.

3. Add the mashed chickpeas, greens, lemon juice, and the remaining whole chickpeas to the mixture in the slow cooker. Stir to blend. For around 30 minutes, simmer the kale on Low with the cover on.

4. Spread the stew evenly among 6 bowls and top with oil. Add basil as a garnish. If desired, garnish with lemon slices.

NUTRITION FACTS (PER SERVING)

Calories: 191	Carbohydrates: 23g	Fat: 8g	Protein: 6g

85. Spinach Ravioli with Artichokes & Olives

Prep Time: 15 minutes

Serves: 4

Beverage Paring: Apricot nectar

You can prepare a healthy dinner in 15 minutes with pre-made spinach ravioli and a few staple cupboard ingredients. To develop a strong flavor quickly, use ingredients like toasted pine nuts, briny Kalamata olives, and oil-packed sun-dried tomatoes. Frozen artichokes can be substituted with a 15-ounce can; just be sure to drain and thoroughly rinse them first.

- ½ cup oil-packed sun-dried tomatoes drained (2 tablespoons oil reserved)
- 2 (8-ounce) packages of refrigerated or frozen spinach-and-ricotta ravioli
- 1 (10-ounce) package of frozen quartered artichoke hearts, thawed
- ¼ cup chopped fresh basil
- ¼ cup Kalamata olives, sliced
- 1 (15-ounce) can of no-salt-added cannellini beans, rinsed
- 3 tablespoons toasted pine nuts

1. Bring the water in a big pot to a boil. Cook ravioli as directed on the package. Drain, then toss with 1 tablespoon of the saved oil.

2. In a big nonstick frypan, heat the last tablespoon of oil over medium heat. Add the beans and artichokes, and cook for three minutes or until cooked through.

3. Add basil, sun-dried tomatoes, olives, cooked ravioli, and pine nuts after folding.

NUTRITION FACTS (PER SERVING)

Calories: 454	Carbohydrates: 61g	Fat: 19g	Protein: 15g

86. Cauliflower Rice Bowls with Grilled Chicken

Prep Time: 30 minutes

Serves: 4

Even though they only require 30 minutes to prepare, these delicious and healthful cauliflower rice bowls with feta, olives, vegetables, and grilled chicken are amazing.

- 4 cups cauliflower rice
- 6 tablespoons and 1 teaspoon extra-virgin olive oil, divided
- ⅓ cup chopped red onion
- ½ cup chopped fresh dill, divided
- ¾ teaspoon salt, divided
- 1 pound boneless, skinless chicken breasts
- 3 tablespoons lemon juice
- ½ teaspoon ground pepper, divided
- 1 teaspoon dried oregano
- 1 cup chopped cucumber
- 1 cup halved cherry tomatoes
- 2 tablespoons chopped Kalamata olives
- 4 wedges Lemon wedges for serving
- 2 tablespoons crumbled feta cheese

1. Warm 2 tbsp of oil in a skillet over medium-high heat. Add 1/4 teaspoon salt, the onion, and the cauliflower. Cook for about five minutes, stirring periodically, or until the cauliflower is tender. Add 1/4 cup dill and turn the heat off.

2. In the meantime, rub a teaspoon of oil all over the chicken. Add a quarter teaspoon each of salt and pepper. Grill for about 15 minutes total, flipping once, or until an instant-read thermometer put into the thickest portion of the breast records 165 degrees F (730C). Slice diagonally.

3. In another small bowl, combine the remaining 4 tablespoons of oil, oregano, lemon juice, and the last 1/4 tsp of salt and pepper.

4. The cauliflower rice should be divided into 4 dishes. Add the feta, tomatoes, cucumber, olives, and chicken on top. Add the final 1/4 cup of dill. Use the vinaigrette as a drizzle. If desired, garnish with lemon slices.

NUTRITION FACTS (PER SERVING)

Calories: 411	Carbohydrates: 10g	Fat: 28g	Protein: 29g

(V) (vg)

87. Crispy Baked Ravioli with Red Pepper & Mushroom Bolognese

Prep Time: 20 minutes

Cook Time: 15 minutes

Serves: 4

According to legend, a St. Louis cook invented toasted ravioli by placing the pasta in hot oil rather than water. By baking the dish in place of frying it and including a serving of vegetables in the shape of a vegetarian Bolognese sauce, we lighten it up in this case. More good news: it just takes 35 minutes to prepare this quick vegetarian meal.

- 1 ½ cups chopped yellow onions
- 2 tablespoons extra-virgin olive oil
- 1 cup chopped carrots
- 2 tablespoons no-salt-added tomato paste
- 3 cloves garlic, minced
- 4 cups of reduced-sodium vegetable broth
- 1 (15-ounce) can of no-salt-added cannellini beans, rinsed
- 1 cup water
- 1 cup mixed dry lentils (brown, green, and black)
- ¾ teaspoon salt
- ½ cup chopped sun-dried tomatoes in oil drained
- ½ teaspoon ground pepper
- 1 ½ teaspoons red-wine vinegar
- 1 tablespoon of chopped fresh dill, plus more for garnish

1. Set the oven to 425 Fahrenheit (2180C). Cooking spray should be applied before setting a wire rack on the baking sheet with a rim.

2. In a dish, mix Parmesan, breadcrumbs, and Italian seasoning. In a different shallow dish, whisk together the egg and water. Dip the ravioli in the egg, letting the excess drip off, before coating it in the breadcrumb mixture and pressing to set. Place it on the wire rack. Spray cooking oil on the ravioli sparingly.

3. Bake the ravioli for about 15 minutes, or until crisp and golden.

4. In the meantime, warm the oil in a large pan over medium-high heat. Add the bell pepper and mushrooms, and stir-fry for 4 minutes or until the vegetables are tender. Add the walnuts and whisk for a minute. About 2 minutes later, add the marinara and heat it through.

5. If desired, top the ravioli with additional Parmesan and serve with the sauce.

NUTRITION FACTS (PER SERVING)

Calories: 479	Carbohydrates: 49g	Fat: 23g	Protein: 20g

88. Prosciutto Pizza with Corn & Arugula

Prep Time: 20 minutes

Serves: 4

Beverage Paring: Iced lemon balm tea

This prosciutto and arugula pizza that is grilled is the ideal summertime dinner. For this 20-minute healthy pizza recipe, if you have the opportunity, let the dough rest at room temperature for ten minutes to make rolling out easier. Fresh corn can be substituted with frozen; simply pat the corn dry before sprinkling it on the pie.

- 2 tablespoons extra-virgin olive oil, divided
- 1-pound pizza dough, preferably whole-wheat
- 1 clove garlic, minced
- 1 cup fresh corn kernels
- 1 cup part-skim shredded mozzarella cheese
- 1 ounce very thinly sliced prosciutto, torn into 1-inch pieces
- ½ cup torn fresh basil
- 1 ½ cups arugula
- ¼ teaspoon ground pepper

1. Set the grill to medium-high heat. (Or, you could bake.)

2. On a dusted surface, roll out the dough into a 12-inch oval. Transfer to a sizable baking sheet that has been lightly dusted with flour. In a bowl, mix 1 tbs of oil and the garlic. Bring the cheese, corn, prosciutto, cheese, and garlic oil to the grill.

3. Oil the grill rack. Place the grill on the crust. Grill the dough for one to two minutes or until it is puffy and lightly browned.

4. Spread the garlic oil over the top of the crust. Add cheese, corn, and prosciutto on top. For a further 2 to 3 minutes, grill the covered dish until the cheese is melted and the bottom crust is just starting to brown. The pizza should be put back on the baking sheet.

5. Add pepper, basil, and arugula to the pizza's toppings. Add the final 1 tablespoon of oil in a drizzle.

NUTRITION FACTS (PER SERVING)

Calories: 436	Carbohydrates: 53g	Fat: 20g	Protein: 18g

V **gf** **vg**

89. Vegan Lentil Soup

Prep
Time:
20 minutes

Serves:
6

This vegan lentil soup dish is brimming with fresh ingredients with plenty of lentils that provide a healthy dose of fiber in every meal. This vegan soup is a healthy dinner or ideal lunch for the winter that the whole family will enjoy.

- 1 ½ cups chopped yellow onions
- 2 tablespoons extra-virgin olive oil
- 1 cup chopped carrots
- 2 tablespoons no-salt-added tomato paste
- 3 cloves garlic, minced
- 4 cups of reduced-sodium vegetable broth
- 1 (15-ounce) can of no-salt-added cannellini beans, rinsed
- 1 cup water
- 1 cup mixed dry lentils (brown, green, and black)
- ¾ teaspoon salt
- ½ cup chopped sun-dried tomatoes in oil drained
- ½ teaspoon ground pepper
- 1 ½ teaspoons red-wine vinegar
- 1 tablespoon of chopped fresh dill, plus more for garnish

1. Warm the oil in a big, medium-heat, heavy pot. Add the onions and carrots; simmer for 3 to 4 minutes, stirring periodically, until tender. Cook the garlic for approximately a minute, stirring regularly, until fragrant. Cook the mixture with the tomato paste while constantly stirring for approximately a minute or until it is thoroughly coated.

2. Add salt, pepper, sun-dried tomatoes, cannellini beans, lentils, broth, and water. Boil, then reduce the heat to maintain a simmer. For 30 to 40 minutes, cook the lentils with the cover on.

3. Add vinegar and dill after taking the pan off the heat. If desired, add more dill to the garnish before serving.

NUTRITION FACTS (PER SERVING)

| Calories: 272 | Carbohydrates: 42g | Fat: 7g | Protein: 13g |

90. Green Shakshuka with Spinach, Chard & Feta

Prep Time: 30 minutes

Serves: 6

Beverage Paring: Carrot and ginger juice

This green shakshuka dish was inspired by HaBasta, a well-known eatery on the outskirts of Tel Aviv's Carmel Market. There, the shakshuka is stuffed with green chard and spinach, while a dash of hot pepper adds just the right amount of heat. For a quick meal or brunch, serve the dish with pita or crusty bread to mop up the sauce.

- 1 large onion, finely chopped
- ⅓ cup extra-virgin olive oil
- 12 ounces`1s chard, stemmed and chopped
- ½ cup dry white wine (or Apple cider vinegar)
- 12 ounces mature spinach, stemmed and chopped
- 1 small serrano pepper or jalapeño, thinly sliced
- ¼ teaspoon kosher salt
- 2 medium cloves garlic, very thinly sliced
- ¼ teaspoon ground pepper
- ½ cup crumbled feta or goat cheese
- 2 tablespoons unsalted butter
- ½ cup low-sodium, no-chicken or chicken broth
- 6 large eggs

1. Heat the oil in a big skillet. Add the onion and sauté it for 7 to 8 minutes, stirring frequently, until it is tender and translucent but not browned.

2. Add spinach and chard, a few handfuls at a time, and simmer for about 5 minutes, stirring frequently, until wilted. Wine, jalapeno (or serrano), garlic, salt, and pepper should be added. Cook, stirring regularly, for 2 to 4 minutes or until the wine is absorbed and the garlic softens. Cook, stirring, until some of the liquid is absorbed and the butter is melted, 1 to 2 minutes after adding the broth and butter.

3. Scatter eggs on top of the vegetables. For 3 to 5 minutes, or until the whites are set, cook covered over medium-low heat. Once the cheese has been added, turn off the heat, cover the pan, and let it stand for two minutes before serving.

NUTRITION FACTS (PER SERVING)

| Calories: 296 | Carbohydrates: 9g | Fat: 23g | Protein: 11g |

91. BBQ Shrimp with Garlicky Kale and Parmesan-Herb Couscous

Prep Time: 20 minutes

Serves: 4

Since it has already been partially cooked, dry whole-wheat couscous is a popular quick-cooking whole-grain dish on weekdays in the United States. You can also make this nutritious dinner quickly by purchasing peeled shrimp, a bag of already-chopped kale, and a bottle of barbecue sauce.

- ¼ teaspoon poultry seasoning
- 1 cup low-sodium chicken broth
- ⅔ cup whole-wheat couscous
- 1 tablespoon butter
- ⅓ cup grated Parmesan cheese
- 3 tablespoons extra-virgin olive oil, divided
- ¼ cup water
- 8 cups chopped kale
- ¼ cup barbecue sauce
- 1 large clove of garlic, smashed
- ¼ teaspoon salt
- ¼ teaspoon crushed red pepper
- 1-pound raw shrimp (26-30 per pound), peeled and deveined

1. Place the lemon juice and tahini in the bowl of a food processor and process for 1 minute. After scraping down the bottom and sides of the bowl, process for an extra 30 seconds. This additional time is used to "whip" or "cream" the tahini, resulting in smooth and creamy hummus.

2. Mix the whipped tahini and lemon juice with the olive oil, cumin, minced garlic, and 1/2 teaspoon salt; after scraping the bowl's bottom and sides, process for a further 30 seconds or until everything is thoroughly mixed. Open, rinse, and drain the chickpeas. Fill the food processor with half the chickpeas. Take one minute to process. The remaining chickpeas should be added to the bowl after cleaning the sides and bottom and processed for one to two minutes or until thick and extremely smooth.

3. The hummus will probably be overly thick or contain little chickpea pieces. If this happens, fix it by gradually adding 2 to 3 tablespoons of water while the food processor is running until the appropriate consistency is reached.

4. After tasting, adjust the salt as necessary. Olive oil and paprika should be drizzled over the hummus before serving. Homemade hummus should be kept in the refrigerator for up to a week in an airtight container.

NUTRITION FACTS (PER SERVING)

Calories: 414	Carbohydrates: 36g	Fat: 17g	Protein: 32g

92. One-Skillet Salmon with Fennel & Sun-Dried Tomato Couscous

Prep Time: 30 minutes

Serves: 4

In this nutritious one-pan meal recipe, lemon and sun-dried tomato pesto season both the salmon and the couscous. If preferred, top the salmon with a dollop of plain yoghurt and additional lemon wedges.

- 1 ¼ pounds salmon, skinned and cut into 4 portions
- 1 lemon
- ¼ teaspoon salt
- 4 tablespoons sun-dried tomato pesto, divided
- ¼ teaspoon ground pepper
- 2 tablespoons extra-virgin olive oil, divided
- 1 cup couscous, preferably whole-wheat
- 2 cloves garlic, sliced
- 2 medium fennel bulbs, cut into half-inch wedges; fronds reserved
- 3 scallions, sliced
- ¼ cup sliced green olives
- 1 ½ cups low-sodium chicken broth
- 2 tablespoons toasted pine nuts

1. Zest a lemon, saving the zest. The lemon should be cut into 8 wedges. Add 1 1/2 teaspoons of pesto to each piece of salmon after seasoning it with salt and pepper.

2. Warm 1 tb of oil in a skillet over medium-high heat. Add half of the fennel and heat for 2 to 3 minutes, or until the bottom is browned. Place on a platter. Repeat with the rest of the 1 tbsp of oil and fennel, lowering the heat to medium. Toss onto a platter. Add the couscous and scallions to the pan and toss constantly for 1 to 2 minutes, or until the couscous is lightly toasted. Add the remaining 2 tablespoons of pesto along with the broth, olives, pine nuts, garlic, and lemon zest that were set aside.

3. Fold the fish and fennel into the couscous. Add the lemon slices on top of the fish. Reduce heat to medium-low, cover the pan, and cook for 10 to 14 minutes, or until the salmon is cooked through and the couscous is soft. If desired, add fennel fronds as a garnish.

NUTRITION FACTS (PER SERVING)

Calories: 543	Carbohydrates: 46g	Fat: 24g	Protein: 38g

93. Chicken & Spinach Skillet Pasta with Lemon & Parmesan

Prep Time: 25 minutes

Serves: 4

This one-pan chicken pasta dish combines sautéed spinach and lean chicken breast for a one-bowl meal that is garlicky, lemony and tastes best with a sprinkle of Parmesan cheese on top. In any case, it's a simple and quick weekday dish that I enjoy so much. I still make it every week for dinner. The whole family will enjoy this simple dinner.

- 2 tablespoons extra-virgin olive oil
- 8 ounces' gluten-free penne pasta or whole-wheat penne pasta
- 1 pound of skinless, boneless chicken breast or thighs, trimmed, if necessary, and sliced into bite-size pieces
- ¼ teaspoon ground pepper
- ½ teaspoon salt
- 4 cloves garlic, minced
- 4 tablespoons grated Parmesan cheese, divided
- Juice and zest of 1 lemon
- ½ cup dry white wine (or Apple cider vinegar)
- 10 cups chopped fresh spinach

1. Prepare the pasta as directed on the package. Drain, then set apart.

2. In the meantime, warm the oil in a sizable, high-sided skillet over high heat. Cook, stirring frequently, for seven minutes, until the chicken is just cooked through. Add chicken, salt, and pepper. Add the garlic and stir-fry for approximately a minute, or until fragrant. Add wine, lemon juice, and zest; simmer after stirring.

3. Turn off the heat. Add cooked pasta and spinach to the mixture. As soon as the spinach has just begun to wilt, cover and leave. Distribute among 4 plates, adding 1 tablespoon of Parmesan to each portion.

NUTRITION FACTS (PER SERVING)

Calories: 335	Carbohydrates: 25g	Fat: 12g	Protein: 29g

94. Sheet-Pan Chicken Thighs with Brussels Sprouts & Gnocchi

Prep Time: 20 minutes

Cook Time: 10 minutes

Serves: 4

This quick and simple dinner dish roasts chicken thighs, Brussels sprouts, cherry tomatoes, and boxed gnocchi on the same sheet pan for a complete meal. Despite being simple, this recipe has a ton of flavor because of the ingredients like red wine vinegar, oregano, and garlic. Everything comes together to create a dish that is ready for heavy rotation on weeknights in your home

- 2 tablespoons chopped fresh oregano, divided
- 4 tablespoons extra-virgin olive oil, divided
- 2 large cloves garlic, minced and divided
- ¼ teaspoon salt, divided
- ½ teaspoon ground pepper, divided
- 1 pound Brussels sprouts, trimmed and quartered
- 1 cup sliced red onion
- 1 (16-ounce) package of shelf-stable gnocchi
- 4 boneless, skinless chicken thighs, trimmed
- 1 tablespoon red-wine vinegar (or red grape juice)
- 1 cup halved cherry tomatoes

1. Set the oven to 450 degrees Fahrenheit (3220C).

2. In a big bowl, combine 1 tablespoon oregano, 2 tablespoons oil, half the garlic, 1/8 teaspoon salt, and 1/4 teaspoon pepper. Add the onion, gnocchi, and Brussels sprouts and mix to combine. Spread out on a big baking sheet with a rim.

3. In the big bowl, combine 1 tablespoon oil, the remaining 1 tablespoon garlic, the remaining 1 tablespoon of oregano, the remaining 1/8 teaspoon salt, and the remaining 1/4 tp pepper. Chicken should be added and coated. Place the chicken inside the combination of vegetables. Roast for ten minutes.

4. After taking the dish out of the oven, toss in the tomatoes. Roast the chicken for another 10 minutes or so, or until it is just cooked through and the Brussels sprouts are soft. The vegetable mixture should be mixed with vinegar and the final tablespoon of oil.

NUTRITION FACTS (PER SERVING)

Calories: 604	Carbohydrates: 61g	Fat: 24g	Protein: 39g

95. Quinoa, Avocado & Chickpea Salad over Mixed Greens

Prep Time: 20 minutes

Serves: 2

Beverage Paring: Chia Seed Smoothie

With avocado and quinoa, this superfood vegan chickpea salad is low in cholesterol, high in protein, and seasoned with a simple lime dressing. Perfect for any season when you need to refuel with meals that are high in nutrients. Serve it as a side dish or as a small lunch or dinner.

- ⅓ cup quinoa
- ⅔ cup water
- ¼ teaspoon kosher salt or other coarse salt
- 2 teaspoons grated lemon zest
- 1 clove garlic, crushed and peeled
- 3 tablespoons lemon juice
- ¼ teaspoon ground pepper
- 3 tablespoons olive oil
- 1 cup rinsed, no-salt-added canned chickpeas
- ½ avocado, diced
- 1 medium carrot, shredded (1/2 cup)
- 1 (5-ounce) package of prewashed mixed greens, such as baby kale-spinach blend (8 cups packed) or spring mix

1. In a small pan, bring water to a boil. Add the quinoa and stir. Turn down the heat to low, cover the pan, and simmer for 15 minutes or until all the liquid has been absorbed. Fluff and use a fork to separate the grains; allow to cool for five minutes.

2. In the meantime, salt the garlic on the chopping board. Use the side of a spoon to smash the garlic until a paste forms. Scrape into a medium bowl. Add pepper, oil, lemon juice, and zest to the mixture. 3 Tbsp. of the dressing should be transferred to a small bowl and put aside.

3. Add the remaining dressing to the bowl along with the chickpeas, carrot, and avocado. Gently mix to blend. To allow flavors to meld, allow them to stand for 5 minutes. Toss the quinoa gently to coat it after adding it.

4. Add the greens to a large bowl and mix with the 3 Tbsp. dressing that was set aside. Place the greens on two plates, then add the quinoa mixture on top.

NUTRITION FACTS (PER SERVING)

Calories: 501	Carbohydrates: 47g	Fat: 32g	Protein: 12g

96. Caprese Stuffed Portobello Mushrooms

Prep Time: 25 minutes

Cook Time: 15 minutes

Serves: 4

To create a tasty and filling vegetarian main dish, we took the essential components of the well-known Caprese salad—tomatoes, fresh mozzarella, and basil—and stacked them into portobello mushroom caps

- 1 medium clove garlic, minced
- 3 tablespoons extra-virgin olive oil, divided
- ½ teaspoon salt, divided
- 4 portobello mushrooms (about 14 ounces), stems and gills removed
- ½ teaspoon ground pepper, divided
- 1 cup halved cherry tomatoes
- ½ cup thinly sliced fresh basil
- ½ cup fresh mozzarella pearls, drained and patted dry
- 2 teaspoons of the best-quality balsamic vinegar

1. Turn on the oven to 400 F (2040C).

2. Combine 2 tablespoons oil, 2 cloves of garlic, 1/4 tsp salt, and 1/4 tsp pepper in a small bowl. Apply the oil mixture all over the mushrooms using a silicone brush. Place the mushrooms on a large baking sheet with a rim and bake for 10 minutes, or until mostly soft.

3. In the meantime, combine the tomatoes, mozzarella, basil, and the remaining 1/4 teaspoon pepper, salt, and oil in a medium bowl. Remove the mushrooms from the oven once they have softened, then fill them with the tomato mixture. Bake for about 12 to 15 minutes in the oven, or until the tomatoes have wilted and the cheese has completely melted. Add half a teaspoon of vinegar to each mushroom before serving.

NUTRITION FACTS (PER SERVING)

Calories: 186	Carbohydrates: 6g	Fat: 16g	Protein: 6g

97. Spicy & Sweet Roasted Salmon with Wild Rice Pilaf

Prep Time: 15 minutes

Cook Time: 15 minutes

Serves: 4

Beverage Paring: Sparkling Pomegranate Water

This quick and simple roasted salmon meal gets its heat from fresh jalapenos and its sweetness from honey and balsamic vinegar. This nutritious dinner comes together in just 30 minutes and is finished with a wild rice pilaf that has a nutty flavor.

- 2 tablespoons of balsamic vinegar
- 5 skinless salmon fillets, frozen or fresh (1 1/4 lbs.)
- 1 tablespoon of honey
- ⅛ teaspoon of ground pepper
- ¼ teaspoon of salt
- 1 cup of chopped red and/or yellow bell pepper
- 2 scallions (green parts only), thinly sliced
- 2 ⅔ cups of Wild Rice Pilaf
- ½ to 1 small jalapeño pepper, finely chopped and seeded
- ¼ cup of chopped fresh Italian parsley

1. Set the oven to 425 degrees Fahrenheit (2180C). A 15 by 10-inch baking pan should be lined with parchment paper. Put the salmon in the ready-to-use pan. Pour half of the mixture over the salmon after whisking the vinegar and honey together in a small bowl. Add salt and pepper to taste.

2. Roast the salmon for about 15 minutes, or until the thickest section flakes easily. Add a last drizzle of the vinegar mixture.

3. Spray cooking spray into a 10-inch nonstick skillet and heat it over medium heat. Jalapeno and bell pepper should be added. Cook, stirring frequently, for five minutes or until just tender. Turn off the heat. Add the scallion greens and stir.

4. Sprinkle the pepper mixture and parsley on top of the four salmon fillets. Serve alongside pilaf.

NUTRITION FACTS (PER SERVING)

Calories: 339	Carbohydrates: 43g	Fat: 5g	Protein: 30g

98. Eggplant Parmesan

Prep Time: 15 minutes

Cook Time: 20 minutes

Serves: 6

In this simple eggplant Parmesan recipe, layers of breaded, crispy eggplant slices are baked rather than fried. It's impossible not to enjoy the combination of mozzarella, Parmesan, tomato sauce, and crunchy bread crumbs!

- 2 large eggs
- Canola or olive oil cooking spray
- 2 tablespoons water
- ¾ cup grated Parmesan cheese, divided
- 1 cup panko breadcrumbs
- 1 teaspoon Italian seasoning
- ½ teaspoon salt
- 2 medium eggplants (around 2 pounds total), cut crosswise into ¼-inch-thick slices
- ½ teaspoon ground pepper
- ¼ cup fresh basil leaves, torn
- 1 (24-ounce) jar of no-salt-added tomato sauce
- 2 cloves garlic, grated
- 1 cup shredded part-skim mozzarella cheese, divided
- ½ teaspoon crushed red pepper

1. Set the lower and middle oven rack positions, and preheat the oven to 400°F (2040C). Spray cooking oil on two baking sheets and a 9 by 13-inch baking dish.

2. In a wide bowl, stir together the eggs and water. In a different small bowl, combine breadcrumbs, 1/4 cup Parmesan, and Italian seasoning. Egg mixture first, then breadcrumb mixture, coating eggplant and gently pressing to adhere.

3. Place the eggplant on the preheated baking pans in a single layer. Spray cooking spray liberally on the eggplant's surface on both sides. The eggplant should bake for about 30 minutes, turning it halfway through and transferring the pans between racks. Add salt and pepper to taste.

4. In the meantime, combine tomato sauce with red pepper flakes, garlic, and basil in a bowl.

5. Disperse about 1/2 cup of the sauce in the baking dish that has been prepared. Spread the sauce with half of the eggplant pieces. Sprinkle 1/4 cup Parmesan and 1/2 cup mozzarella over the eggplant after spooning 1 cup of sauce over it. Add the remaining cheese, sauce, and eggplant on top.

6. Bake for about 30 minutes, or until the top is golden and the sauce is bubbling. Allow it to cool for five minutes. If preferred, add additional basil before serving.

NUTRITION FACTS (PER SERVING)

Calories: 241	Carbohydrates: 28g	Fat: 9g	Protein: 14g

99. Zucchini Lasagna Rolls with Smoked Mozzarella

Prep Time: 30 minutes

Cook Time: 20 minutes

Serves: 4

In this nutritious variation on lasagna rolls, zucchini strips are used in place of lasagna noodles to create a family-friendly meal that is packed with vegetables. Allow the youngsters to get their hands messy as they roll the zucchini ribbons in the cheese filling for this recipe. Slice the zucchini rapidly into uniformly thin strips using a vegetable peeler or mandoline to make rolling and cooking easier.

- 2 teaspoons extra-virgin olive oil
- 2 large zucchinis, trimmed
- ½ teaspoon ground pepper, divided
- 8 tablespoons shredded smoked mozzarella cheese, divided
- ¼ teaspoon salt, divided
- 3 tablespoons grated Parmesan cheese, divided
- 1 ⅓ cups part-skim ricotta
- 1 large egg, lightly beaten
- 1 package of frozen spinach, thawed and patted dry
- ¾ cup low-sodium marinara sauce, divided
- 1 clove garlic, minced
- 2 tablespoons chopped fresh basil

1. Arrange the oven's upper and lower racks and preheat to 425 degrees F (2180C). Coat two rimmed baking sheets with cooking spray.

2. Cut the zucchini into 24 strips that are each about 1/8 inch thick by cutting them lengthwise.

3. Combine the oil, 1/4 teaspoon pepper, and 1/8 teaspoon salt in a big bowl with the zucchini. Place the zucchini on the prepared pans in a single layer.

4. Bake the zucchini for about 10 minutes total, rotating once, until soft.

5. In the meantime, mix 1 tablespoon Parmesan and 2 tablespoons mozzarella in a small bowl. Place aside. Mix the remaining 6 tbsps mozzarella, 2 tbsps Parmesan, 1/4 tsp pepper, and 1/8 tsp salt with the egg, ricotta, spinach, and garlic in a medium bowl.

6. Line an 8-inch square baking pan with 1/4 cup marinara. A zucchini strip should have 1 tablespoon of the ricotta mixture placed close to the bottom. Place it seam-side down in the baking dish after rolling it up. Repeat with the rest of the filling and zucchini. The saved cheese mixture should be used to top the rolls with the rest of the 1/2 cup of marinara sauce.

7. Bake the zucchini rolls for about 20 minutes, or until the tops are bubbly and gently browned. Observe for five minutes. Basil should be added just before serving.

NUTRITION FACTS (PER SERVING)

Calories: 315	Carbohydrates: 17g	Fat: 19g	Protein: 22g

100. Chicken with Tomato-Balsamic Pan Sauce

Prep Time: 35 minutes

Serves: 4

Beverage Paring: Lemon water

If you don't have fennel seeds on hand, try cumin or coriander seeds instead, or use 1 tsp of a ground herb or spice. Fennel seeds give this balsamic and tomato sauce an extra bite. To mop up the sauce, serve this simple chicken breast recipe with crusty bread or whole-wheat spaghetti. Store any leftover chicken tenders in your freezer in an airtight container for up to three months. When you have enough, thaw them out for a different use.

- ½ teaspoon salt, divided
- 2 8-ounce boneless, skinless chicken breasts
- ½ teaspoon ground pepper, divided
- 3 tablespoons extra-virgin olive oil, divided
- ¼ cup white whole-wheat flour
- ½ cup halved cherry tomatoes
- ¼ cup balsamic vinegar
- 2 tablespoons sliced shallot
- 1 cup low-sodium chicken broth
- 1 tablespoon fennel seeds, toasted and lightly crushed
- 1 tablespoon minced garlic
- 1 tablespoon butter

1. Take out and save the reserved chicken tenders for further use. Cut each breast in half to create four pieces. With a sizable piece of plastic wrap, place it on a cutting board. Use the bottom of a heavy pot or the smooth side of a meat mallet to pound the material to an equal thickness of about 1/4 inch. Add a quarter teaspoon each of salt and pepper. Shaking off excess flour, coat the cutlets on both sides with flour placed in a shallow dish.

2. Warm 2 tbsps of oil in a large skillet over medium-high heat. Add two pieces of chicken and cook, rotating once, for two to three minutes on each side or until thoroughly browned. Place on a sizable serving plate, cover with foil, and keep warm. Use the leftover chicken in the same way.

3. Add tomatoes, shallots, and the remaining 1 tablespoon of oil to the pan. Stirring occasionally, cook for two minutes or until softened. Bring to a boil after adding vinegar. Cook for around 45 seconds, or until the vinegar is reduced by half, scraping up any browned bits from the pan's bottom as you go. Add the rest of the 1/4 tsp of salt and pepper, the broth, the garlic, and the fennel seeds. Stirring frequently, cook for 4 to 7 minutes, or until the sauce has reduced by roughly half. With the heat off, whisk in the butter. Serve the sauce over the chicken.

NUTRITION FACTS (PER SERVING)

Calories: 294	Carbohydrates: 10g	Fat: 17g	Protein: 25g

101. Roasted Pistachio-Crusted Salmon with Broccoli

Prep Time: 30 minutes

Cook Time: 15 minutes

Serves: 4

Weeknight dinners can be made quickly with this simple one-pan roasted salmon and broccoli dish, which is also sophisticated enough for guests. Other fish or chicken breasts would also taste delicious with the lemony pistachio crust.

- 2 cloves garlic, sliced
- 8 cups of broccoli florets with 2-inch stalks attached
- 3 tablespoons extra-virgin olive oil, divided
- ½ teaspoon ground pepper, divided
- ¾ teaspoon salt, divided
- 1 ¼ pounds of salmon fillet, cut into 4 portions
- ½ cup salted pistachios, coarsely chopped
- Zest 1 medium lemon, plus wedges for serving.
- 2 tablespoons chopped fresh chives
- 4 teaspoons mayonnaise

1. Set the oven to 425 Fahrenheit (2180C). Spray cooking oil on a large baking sheet with a rim.

2. On the prepared baking sheet, mix the garlic, broccoli, 2 tablespoons oil, 1/4 teaspoon pepper, and 1/2 teaspoon salt. Roast for 5 minutes.

3. In the meantime, combine in a separate bowl the pistachios, chives, lemon zest, remaining 1 tablespoon oil, and 1/4 teaspoon each of pepper and salt. Each portion of salmon should have 1 teaspoon of mayonnaise spread over it before the pistachio mixture is added.

4. Move the broccoli to one side of the baking sheet, leaving the other side empty, and arrange the salmon there. Roast for a further 8 to 15 minutes, depending on thickness, until the broccoli is just soft and the salmon is opaque in the center. If desired, garnish with lemon slices.

NUTRITION FACTS (PER SERVING)

Calories: 424	Carbohydrates: 12g	Fat: 27g	Protein: 36g

102. Pan-Seared Halibut with Creamed Corn & Tomatoes

Prep Time: 40 minutes

Serves: 4

Beverage Paring: Green Tea

You steep corncobs in milk for this nutritious fish dish; the resulting "stock" increases the flavor of creamed corn made from scratch, and extra corn starch helps to give the dish its thick texture. Halibut is called for in this recipe; you can substitute Pacific cod or tilapia raised in the United States as an alternative. Serve this refreshing concoction of grilled fish, corn, tomatoes, and basil to company on the weekends or to your family on weeknights.

- 1 ½ cups whole milk
- 4 ears of corn, husked
- 3 cloves garlic, divided
- 3 cups chopped tomatoes
- 1 sprig of fresh thyme
- 3 tablespoons chopped fresh basil
- ¾ teaspoon salt, divided
- 2 tablespoons extra-virgin olive oil, divided
- 1 tablespoon butter
- 2 tablespoons all-purpose flour
- ¼ cup chopped shallot
- 2 tablespoons grated Parmesan cheese
- 1 ¼ pounds halibut, cut into 4 portions
- ½ teaspoon ground pepper, divided

1. Remove the corn's kernels and set them aside. Place the cobs in a big saucepan after cutting or breaking them in half. Add milk, thyme, and two garlic cloves. Cook until the edges are beginning to simmer over medium heat. Take the pot off the heat, cover it, and soak for 10 minutes. Discard the sediments after straining them into a glass measuring cup or small bowl.

2. Grate the last garlic clove into a medium bowl in the meantime. Stir in 1 tablespoon oil, 1/4 teaspoon salt, tomatoes, and basil. Place aside.

3. Melt the butter over low heat in the pan. Shallots should be added and cooked for about a minute, stirring regularly, until tender. Then, add the saved corn kernels and simmer for about 3 minutes, stirring regularly, until they start to soften. Add flour, then cook for 30 seconds. Add the milk slowly while stirring. Set the heat control to a simmer, cover, and cook for 5 minutes or until thickened. Add Parmesan, along with 1/4 teaspoon of salt and pepper. Cover and leave out.

4. Add the rest of the 1/4 teaspoon of salt and pepper to the halibut. A sizable nonstick skillet with the remaining 1 tablespoon of oil must be heated over medium-high heat. Add the halibut and cook for 5 to 7 minutes, flipping once, or until just barely cooked through.

5. Arrange the tomatoes and creamed corn on a plate with the halibut.

NUTRITION FACTS (PER SERVING)

Calories: 422	Carbohydrates: 35g	Fat: 17g	Protein: 35g

103. Greek-Inspired Burgers with Herb-Feta Sauce

Prep Time: 25 minutes

Serves: 4

With the addition of a yogurt sauce flavored with feta cheese, oregano, and lemon, these nutritious burgers take on a Mediterranean flair. If you are having trouble finding ground lamb, you may ask the butcher to grind some for you.

- ¼ cup crumbled feta cheese
- 1 cup nonfat plain Greek yogurt
- 3 tablespoons chopped fresh oregano, divided
- 2 teaspoons lemon juice
- ¼ teaspoon lemon zest
- ¾ teaspoon salt, divided
- 1-pound ground lamb or ground beef
- 1 small red onion
- ½ teaspoon ground pepper
- 1 cup sliced cucumber
- 2 whole-wheat pitas, halved, split, and warmed
- 1 plum tomato, sliced

1. Turn the broiler or grill to high or medium heat.

2. In a separate bowl, combine yogurt, feta, 1 tablespoon oregano, lemon juice, lemon zest, and 1/4 teaspoon salt.

3. To create 1/4 cup, slice an onion into 1/4-inch-thick slices. To create another 1/4 cup, add extra onion and finely chop. (Save any leftover onions for different use.) Mix the remaining 2 tablespoons of oregano, together with 1/2 teaspoons each of salt and pepper, with the meat and chopped onion in a large bowl. Form into 4 by 3-inch oval patties.

4. Grill or broil (cook) the burgers, rotating once, for 4 to 6 minutes per side or until an instant-read thermometer reads 160 degrees F (710C). Serve the sauce, onion slices, cucumber, and tomato in pita half sandwiches.

NUTRITION FACTS (PER SERVING)

Calories: 375	Carbohydrates: 24g	Fat: 18g	Protein: 30g

104. Easy Pea & Spinach Carbonara

Prep Time: 20 minutes

Serves: 4

Fresh pasta is a necessity for quick weeknight dinners like this decadent yet healthful dish since it cooks more quickly than dried pasta. The creamy sauce's foundation is an egg base. If you'd like, you can use pasteurized in-shell eggs because they don't become totally cooked.

- ½ cup panko breadcrumbs, preferably whole-wheat
- 1 ½ tablespoons extra-virgin olive oil
- 1 small clove garlic, minced
- 3 tablespoons finely chopped fresh parsley
- 8 tablespoons grated Parmesan cheese, divided
- 3 large egg yolks
- ½ teaspoon ground pepper
- 1 large egg
- ¼ teaspoon salt
- 8 cups baby spinach
- 1 (9-ounce) package of fresh tagliatelle or linguine
- 1 cup peas (fresh or frozen)

1. Fill a big saucepan with 10 cups of water, and boil.

2. In the meantime, warm up some oil in a big skillet over medium-high heat. Garlic and breadcrumbs should be added, and they should be cooked for 2 minutes while stirring constantly. Add 2 tablespoons of Parmesan and the parsley to the small bowl after transfer. Place aside.

3. In a bowl, mix the remaining 6 tablespoons of Parmesan, the egg yolks, the pepper, and the salt.

4. Boil the pasta for one minute while stirring occasionally. Cook the pasta for another minute or so, stirring in the spinach and peas, until it is soft. ¼ cup of cooking water should be set aside. Drain and place in a big bowl.

5. Gradually whisk the egg mixture with the cooking water that was set aside. Toss the spaghetti with tongs as you gradually add the ingredients to blend. Serve with the breadcrumb mixture that was set aside on top.

NUTRITION FACTS (PER SERVING)

Calories: 430	Carbohydrates: 54g	Fat: 15g	Protein: 20g

105. Sheet-Pan Roasted Salmon & Vegetables

Prep Time: 20 minutes **Cook Time:** 15 minutes **Serves:** 4

This Sheet Pan Baked Salmon with Vegetables is a quick, wholesome, and delectable dinner option when you're short on time and meal inspiration. It uses a sheet pan, often known as a baking sheet, with a rimmed edge, which is one of our all-time favorite kitchen appliances, which is why we adore it. This recipe is flavorful and goes great with a Mediterranean diet.

- 2 tablespoons olive oil
- 1-pound fingerling potatoes, halved lengthwise
- 5 garlic cloves, coarsely chopped
- ½ teaspoon freshly ground black pepper
- ½ teaspoon sea salt
- 4, 5 to 6-ounce fresh or frozen skinless salmon fillets
- 2 cups cherry tomatoes
- 2 medium yellow, red, and/or orange sweet peppers cut into rings
- 1 ½ cups chopped fresh parsley (1 bunch)
- 1 Tbsp. dried oregano, crushed, or ¼ cup finely snipped fresh oregano
- ¼ cup pitted kalamata olives, halved
- 1 lemon

1. Set the oven to 425 Fahrenheit (2180C). Add potatoes to a sizable bowl. Toss to coat with 1 Tbsp. oil, 1/8 tsp. salt and black pepper, garlic, and 1 Tbsp. of oil. Wrap in foil and transfer to a 15x10-inch baking tray. Roast for 30 minutes.

2. Thaw any frozen salmon in the meantime. Sweet peppers, tomatoes, parsley, olives, oregano, and 1/8 tsp each of salt and black pepper should all be combined in the same bowl. Add the final 1 Tbsp. of oil and drizzle, then toss to coat.

3. Rinse and dry the salmon. Add the final 1/4 tsp. of salt and black pepper. Salmon should be placed on top of the sweet pepper mixture and potatoes. Roast for 10 more minutes, uncovered, or until salmon flakes.

4. Trim the lemon's zest. Lemon juice should be squeezed over the fish and vegetables. Add a little zest.

NUTRITION FACTS (PER SERVING)

Calories: 422	Carbohydrates: 32g	Fat: 19g	Protein: 33g

DESSERT RECIPES

CHAPTER SIX

DESSERT RECIPES

What makes the Mediterranean diet so wonderful? There are no forbidden food groups or severe limitations, and that includes dessert. You may have your cake and eat it too since this well-liked dietary strategy emphasizes including healthy fruits, fats, vegetables, nuts, and low-fat dairy. (And no, it doesn't have to taste like "diet food," which are foods that resemble sweets but don't really satisfy desires.) I'll show you how: Try one of these Mediterranean diet desserts (such as lemon bars, brownie bites, or avocado chocolate mousse), none of which will throw your diet off course.

106. Avocado Chocolate Mousse

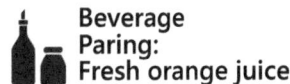

Prep Time: 5 minutes

Serves: 4

Beverage Paring: Fresh orange juice

Here is the recipe for the lovely Brooklyn restaurant's very first dessert: avocado chocolate mousse. The treat is dairy-free, vegan, incredibly rich, creamy, and chocolaty. And, in case you're still wondering, no, it doesn't taste at all like an avocado.
You can prepare the mousse ahead of time and keep it in the refrigerator for up to two days in a resealable container.

- 1-pound dairy-free dark chocolate, preferably 60% cacao, coarsely chopped
- canned coconut milk or 1¼ cups unsweetened almond milk
- 4 small ripe avocados—pitted, peeled and chopped
- 1 tablespoon finely grated orange zest
- ¼ cup agave syrup
- 2 tablespoons puffed quinoa
- 2 teaspoons Aleppo pepper flakes
- 2 teaspoons Maldon sea salt
- 1 tablespoon extra-virgin olive oil

1. Heat the almond or coconut milk in a small saucepan over medium-high heat until an instant-read thermometer reads 175°F (790C). Chop the chocolate, remove from the fire, and mix until smooth. Allow to cool to room temperature.

2. Place the avocados, agave, orange zest, and chilled chocolate mixture in a blender and blend on high until smooth.

3. Distribute the mousse among four bowls for serving. Puffed quinoa, sea salt, Aleppo pepper, and olive oil should all be uniformly distributed.

NUTRITION FACTS (PER SERVING)

Calories: 596	Carbohydrates: 92g	Fat: 42g	Protein: 26g

107. Orange Flower Olive Oil Cake

Prep Time: 40 minutes

Cook Time: 35 minutes

Serves: Make one 8-inch cake

The cake definitely doesn't come to mind when you hear the words "less than an hour" or "doesn't require special equipment," do you agree? After sampling this lovely and simple orange flower olive oil cake, your perspective will change. It pairs well with any kind of seasonal fresh fruit that has been mildly sweetened. It comes out with the ideal amount of sponginess and lasts for days. If it lasts that long, the next day might even be better. You don't even need a mixer to quickly make this simple cake.

- Grated zest of 1 lemon, orange, or Meyer lemon
- 1 cup plus 2 tablespoons (160g) all-purpose flour
- ¾ cup (150g) granulated sugar
- ½ teaspoon kosher salt
- 1 teaspoon baking soda
- 1 extra-large egg
- ⅓ cup (80ml) extra-virgin olive oil
- ¾ cup (180ml) buttermilk
- 1 teaspoon orange flower water, optional
- Fresh berries or sliced fresh stone fruits, optional, for serving
- Confectioners' sugar, as needed

1. Place a rack in the middle of the oven and heat it to 325 degrees Fahrenheit (1620C). An 8-inch cake pan should be lightly greased and lined with parchment paper.

2. Mix the flour, zest, sugar, baking soda, and salt in a medium bowl.

3. Mix the egg, buttermilk, olive oil, and orange blossom water, if using, in a separate bowl by whisking the ingredients together.

4. After adding the buttermilk mixture, incorporate the flour mixture by pouring it over the top and stirring. Utilizing a spatula, scrape the batter into the prepared pan.

5. Bake for 30 to 35 minutes, or until the cake is brown and the top lightly bounces back on your fingertip.

6. Let the cake cool for ten minutes in the pan. After carefully inverting the pan onto a rack and removing the parchment paper, run a knife around the pan's edge. Let the cake finish cooling.

7. Top the cake with fresh fruit or serve it plain and dusted with confectioners' sugar.

NUTRITION FACTS (PER SERVING)

| Calories: 10 | Carbohydrates: 49g | Fat: 10g | Protein: 5g |

108. Peaches-and-cream Ice Pops

Prep Time: 15 minutes **Cook Time:** 2 hours **Serves:** 8

You can pretty much count on us wanting (or eating) an ice pop once the temperature rises above 70 degrees. Additionally, creating your own ice cream is considerably more enjoyable than waiting around for the ice cream truck.

- ⅓ cup (66g) light brown sugar
- 1 pound of peaches, peeled and cut into wedges
- ½ teaspoon ground cinnamon
- 1½ cups (340g) plain Greek yogurt
- Pinch of fine sea salt
- ½ cup (112g) crème fraîche
- ¼ teaspoon pure almond extract
- 2 teaspoons pure vanilla extract

1. Set the oven to 375 degrees Fahrenheit (1900C). Place the peaches on a baking sheet in an even layer. Add salt, cinnamon, and brown sugar; blend by tossing.

2. Roast the peaches for 20 to 25 minutes, or until fork-tender. Cool for 15 minutes.

3. Mix the yogurt, crème fraîche, vanilla, and almond extract in a big bowl. About three-quarters of the mixture should be transferred to a container with a pour spout.

4. Combine the remaining yogurt mixture in the bowl with the chilled peaches. Combine the two using a potato masher; it's fine if there are still peach bits.

5. Fill each ice-pop mold with 2 teaspoons of the yogurt mixture. 4 tablespoons of the peach mixture should be added next, and then 4 tablespoons of the yogurt mixture. Alternate the two as before till the molds are full. The layers blending together is acceptable.

6. Insert an ice-pop stick in the middle of each mold before freezing. Freeze for at least two hours until solid.

7. Warm up the molds in water before removing the ice pops. Keep frozen till you are ready to serve.

NUTRITION FACTS (PER SERVING)

Calories: 121	Carbohydrates: 16g	Fat: 5g	Protein: 4g

109. One-ingredient Watermelon Sorbet

Prep Time: 4 hours

Serves: 8

It's once again that time of year. You'll know when you've stopped blow-drying your hair when you seldom wear shoes and when it's been weeks since you've used the oven. The one-ingredient watermelon sorbet we have is an even better way to chill off. We guarantee that, although it seems too good to be true, it is not.

- 1 ripe medium watermelon, peeled, cubed, and seeded

1. On a baking sheet in the same layer, arrange the watermelon cubes. Place the baking sheet in the freezer while the watermelon is frozen solid for around two hours.

2. Put the watermelon cubes in a blender in batches and purée until smooth.

3. Distribute the puree between two loaf pans (or into one large baking dish), pushing it down as you layer more puree on top.

4. Place the baking pans in the freezer. For an additional 1 to 2 hours, freeze until the sorbet is scoopable. Scoop the sorbet into serving bowls and consume it right away.

NUTRITION FACTS (PER SERVING)

| Calories: 170 | Carbohydrates: 43g | Fat: 1g | Protein: 3g |

110. No-bake, Gluten-free Rose Petal Brownies

Prep Time: 2 hrs 15 min

Serves: 8

We typically dislike picking favorites. But these stunning no-bake rose petal brownies—did we mention they're sugar- and vegan-free?—have us fairly smitten. If you enjoy fudge, we are confident that you will adore this decadent chocolate delight that is studded with just the right amount of macadamia nuts and tart-dried cherries. You don't want to order dried rose petals, do you? Rose tea can be scattered on top for the same appearance and flavor.

Base

- 2⅓ cups pitted dates
- Cooking spray, for pan
- 1⅓ cups almonds
- 2 teaspoons pure vanilla extract
- ⅓ cup cocoa powder
- ¼ teaspoon fine sea salt
- 1 cup roughly chopped macadamia nuts
- 1 cup dried cherries

Topping

- ¼ cup maple syrup
- Fresh or dried rose petals for finishing
- ¼ cup cocoa powder
- 2 tablespoons melted coconut oil

1. TO MAKE THE BASE: Spray cooking spray on a baking pan, then cover the bottom with parchment paper.

2. Blend the dates, almonds, cocoa powder, 1 tablespoon of water, vanilla essence, and salt in the food processor until the mixture is smooth. Press the mixture into a uniform layer in the pan after transferring it there.

3. Distribute and lightly press the cherries and macadamia nuts over the base.

4. TO MAKE THE TOPPING: Combine the cocoa powder, coconut oil, and maple syrup in a not-so-big bowl. Pour onto the base, then level out into a layer. Add rose petals as a garnish.

5. Put the pan in the fridge and let it cold for at least two hours. Serve right away or keep in the fridge for up to a week.

NUTRITION FACTS (PER SERVING)

Calories: 531	Carbohydrates: 75g	Fat: 29g	Protein: 7g

111. Baked Pears with Almond Crumble And Maple Syrup

Prep Time: 15 minutes

Cook Time: 20 minutes

Serves: 6

Beverage Paring: Black coffee

Dessert is something you urgently need. This is not the time to go all out with a gourmet pie or a three-layer cake. But you also can't simply set out a bowl of candy. The solution is baked pears with maple syrup and almond crumble. They are quick to put together, stylish, and only take 35 minutes. The best part is that they virtually taste healthy.

Baked Pears

- 2 tablespoons unsalted butter
- 4 pears, halved
- ½ cup maple syrup
- ¼ teaspoon ground cinnamon
- 1 teaspoon pure vanilla extract

Almond Crumble

- ½ cup rolled oats
- 2 tablespoons unsalted butter
- ¼ cup sliced almonds
- 1 tablespoon heavy cream
- 2 tablespoons pure maple syrup
- ½ teaspoon ground cinnamon
- Whipped cream for serving
- ¼ teaspoon fine sea salt

1. TO MAKE THE BAKED PEARS: Set the oven to 400°F (2040C). The seeds should be removed from the core of each pear half using a spoon or a melon baller. Put the pears on a baking sheet covered with parchment paper.

2. Heat the butter in a pot to melt it. Add cinnamon, vanilla essence, and maple syrup after stirring.

3. Liberally brush the pears with the maple syrup mixture all over. The sliced sides of the pears should be pointing downward.

4. Bake the pears for twenty minutes, or until they are soft.

5. TO MAKE THE ALMOND CRUMBLE: Melt the butter in a pot over medium heat while the pears bake. Stir the oats and almonds for about 3 minutes until they begin to smell slightly toasted. Heavy cream and maple syrup are then added, and the mixture is cooked for about 3 minutes or until it slightly thickens. Add salt and cinnamon and stir. Place in a bowl and allow to cool.

6. Top the warm pears with whipped cream and crumbled pie crust.

NUTRITION FACTS (PER SERVING)

Calories: 292	Carbohydrates: 47g	Fat: 12g	Protein: 2g

112. Peanut Butter–Banana Cookies

Prep Time: 20 minutes

Cook Time: 20 minutes

Serves: 14

When you glance at the ingredient list for these cookies, you will never guess how decadent they are. I feel happy cooking these often as a healthy snack because they are vegan and devoid of gluten and processed sugar. Here, the peanut and banana work in perfect harmony with the coconut sugar.

- 2 tablespoons sugar (optional)
- ½ cup (75g) salted roasted peanuts
- 1 cup (240g) unsweetened chunky peanut butter
- ¼ cup finely mashed banana (about 1 medium)
- ⅔ cup (120g) coconut sugar
- 2 tablespoons maple syrup
- ½ teaspoon baking soda
- 2 teaspoons vanilla extract
- ½ teaspoon kosher salt

1. Set the oven to 375 degrees (1900C). Using parchment paper, line two baking pans.

2. Chop the peanuts roughly. Continue slicing the remaining half into really tiny bits while reserving the other half. Put the finely chopped peanuts and sugar (if using) in a small bowl and set aside. Although it is not necessary, the sugar gives the cookies outside a little crunch.

3. Combine the reserved coarsely chopped peanuts, peanut butter, banana, maple syrup, vanilla, baking soda, and salt in a medium bowl. It will be a heavy, sticky dough. Give it 15 minutes to rest. The dough will become a little bit thicker as the baking soda reacts.

4. Spoon 1 heaping tablespoon of dough into the bowl of peanuts that have been finely chopped. To form a ball, roll the dough in your hands after coating it. Repeat with the rest of the dough and place it on a baking sheet. Cookies should be spaced 2 inches apart because they will spread during baking. Slightly flatten each one with your fingertip.

5. Bake the cookies for ten minutes, or until they crack and the edges start to look crispy. Avoid overbaking because the food will continue to dry out as it cools. After ten minutes of cooling on the pan, transfer to a wire rack. The cookies, which are crisp on the outside and chewy on the inside, can be stored in a sealed container for up to five days.

NUTRITION FACTS (PER SERVING)

| Calories: 185 | Carbohydrates: 18g | Fat: 11g | Protein: 5g |

113. Rosé Poached Pears with Ginger and Vanilla

Prep Time: 10 minutes

Serves: 6

We won't fool ourselves: Fruit for dessert is typically a drag, except if it's cooked in a whole bottle of rosé and topped with a lot of whipped cream. Then it becomes the world's best dessert.

- ½ cup sugar
- 1 bottle dry rosé wine (or vegetable broth)
- 1-inch piece of fresh peeled ginger
- 6 pears, peeled
- 1 vanilla bean, split lengthwise
- Whipped cream for serving

1. Simmer the rosé wine, sugar, and ginger in a big pot. Add the vanilla seeds after scraping the pod out. Stir the sugar until it melts.

2. Gently lower the pears into the liquid, making sure they are completely submerged if additional water is required.

3. Simmer for 20 to 25 minutes, or until the pears are quite soft. Pears should be taken out of the liquid and totally cooled.

4. Boil the liquid until it is reduced to about 34 cups of syrupy liquid, then simmer it uncovered.

5. Arrange each pear on a tiny platter before serving. Each pear should receive 2 tablespoons of syrup, and whipped cream should be served right away.

NUTRITION FACTS (PER SERVING)

Calories: 277	Carbohydrates: 49g	Fat: 0g	Protein: 1g

(V) (gf) (vg)

114. Easy Fruit Compote

Prep Time: 15 minutes

Serves: 2

Utilize this simple recipe to learn how to make fruit compote! Fruit can be used to make compote, either fresh or frozen. It tastes great on toast, yogurt, pancakes, waffles, ice cream, and other foods. The compote from the recipe makes roughly 2 cups.

- 2 tablespoons honey or maple syrup
- 1 pound of fresh or frozen fruit
- Dash of salt

1. If you're using fresh strawberries or peaches, slice them into thin pieces. Blueberries and raspberries are small berries that can be used whole. There is no need to defrost or slice frozen fruit before use.

2. Combine your preferred fruit, sweetener, and a pinch of salt in a medium saucepan. Boil the mixture while occasionally stirring over medium-high heat. For fresh fruit, this will take about 5 minutes; for frozen fruit, it will take around 10 minutes.

3. After it boils, turn the heat down to medium. Use a potato masher or serving fork to mash the fruit until it has the right consistency if you're using chunky fruit or want it to be smoother. It will take around 5 minutes of simmering and frequent stirring for the compote to reduce to about half of its initial volume.

4. Turn off the heat and remove the compote. The compote is normally sweet enough for me at this stage, but you can add additional sweetener to taste if you think it needs it. Mash it up a bit more if you want it to be smoother.

5. Before serving, let the compote cool for a while. Before covering and storing leftover compote in the refrigerator for up to 10 days, let it cool completely.

NUTRITION FACTS (PER SERVING)

| Calories: 97 | Carbohydrates: 24g | Fat: 0g | Protein: 0g |

115. 5-minute Greek Yogurt Pumpkin Parfait

Prep Time: 5 minutes

Serves: 6

This velvety-smooth pumpkin parfait is stuffed with soothing fall flavors like cinnamon, nutmeg, almonds, and dark chocolate for a delightful, healthy dessert choice during the holiday season. It's a quick, healthier substitute for pumpkin pie.

- 1 ¼ cup Greek yogurt
- 1 15-ounce can of pumpkin puree or a scant 2 cups of homemade pumpkin puree
- 3-4 tablespoons mascarpone cheese
- ¼ teaspoon nutmeg
- 2 ½ tablespoons brown sugar
- 1 tablespoon vanilla extract
- 1 ½-2 teaspoons ground cinnamon

Parfait Toppings

- Chocolate chips for garnish
- 2 tbsps honey or molasses, more for garnish
- Chopped hazelnuts or walnuts for garnish

1. In a bowl, mix the pumpkin puree, Greek yogurt, and the remaining ingredients, excluding the chocolate chips and nuts. Combine everything and whisk it together until it has the consistency you desire.

2. Taste it and modify the flavor to your preference (For instance, you may add some more brown sugar or molasses to make it sweeter). If you prefer extra cinnamon or nutmeg, you can modify the seasonings.) Stir it again to mix.

3. Spoon the pumpkin-yogurt concoction into tiny (3-ounce) serving glasses or mason jars. Cover and refrigerate for thirty minutes or overnight.

4. When ready to serve, sprinkle chopped hazelnuts or walnuts, chocolate chips, and molasses on top of each. Enjoy!

NUTRITION FACTS (PER SERVING)

Calories: 143	Carbohydrates: 19g	Fat: 4g	Protein: 6g

116. No-bake Vegan Brownies with Chocolate Ganache

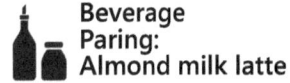

Prep Time: 20 minutes

Serves: 12

Beverage Paring: Almond milk latte

Simple, cacao nib- and walnut-studded raw vegan brownies! For a fudgy, luscious finish, a 5-ingredient coconut oil chocolate ganache is optional but suggested. An improved gluten-free, vegan dessert!

Brownies

- 1 cup raw almonds
- 1 1/2 cups raw walnuts
- 2 1/2 cups dates 2 1/2 cups equal ~15 ounces)
- 2 Tbsp of cacao nibs
- 3/4 cup of cacao powder or unsweetened cocoa powder
- 1/4 tsp sea salt

Ganache Frosting (optional)

- 1 cup dairy-free dark chocolate (chopped)
- 1/4 cup almond milk
- 2 Tbsp coconut oil
- 1/4 tsp sea salt
- 1/4 – 1/2 cup powdered sugar

1. Pulse 1 cup of walnuts and the almonds in a food processor to a nice powder.

2. Add the sea salt and cacao powder, then pulse to mix. Place in a bowl and keep aside.

3. Put the dates in the food processor, then pulse the mixture until only little chunks are left. Take it out and place it aside.

4. Re-add the nut and chocolate mixture to the food processor, and as it runs, add small handfuls of the date pieces via the spout.

5. Continue processing until a dough-like consistency is reached; if the mixture does not hold together when squeezed between your fingers, add more dates. Not all of the dates must be used.

6. Transfer the brownie mixture to a small 8-inch dish lined with parchment paper as directed by the original recipe; make the necessary adjustments if you want to make a smaller or larger batch. Before pressing, stir in the cacao nibs and the remaining 1/2 cup of walnuts that have been roughly chopped. Then apply pressure with your hands until it is hard and flat. To avoid adhering and achieve a really smooth surface, I like to lay down a sheet of plastic wrap.

7. Squeeze the sides of the parchment paper to form a smaller square as you lift the brownies out of the dish, which will make the brownies somewhat denser and thicker.

8. Return to the dish and refrigerate for 10- 15 minutes in the freezer or refrigerator before cutting into 12 squares. Suppose adding ganache, slice later.

9. To make the ganache, heat the almond milk in the microwave for 45 seconds or until it is extremely warm. Alternately, simmer in a small saucepan and then pour into a mixing dish.

10. Immediately stir the chocolate into the warm milk and cover loosely. Allow it to melt for two minutes without touching it.

11. Add salt and mix with a wooden spoon before adding heated coconut oil and mixing with a whisk. Set it in the refrigerator for ten minutes to thicken.

12. Take it out of the fridge and thicken with powdered sugar, adding a bit at a time. Stir once more to mix. Add more tbsps. of powdered sugar; if it's still too thin, then beat until frothy.

13. Drizzle brownies liberally with frosting before garnishing (if desired) with extra raw walnuts and cocoa nibs. Slice into 12 equal squares.

14. To keep brownies fresh, store them in an airtight container. Will keep for three to four days at room temperature or for at least a month in the freezer (but fresh is best).

NUTRITION FACTS (PER SERVING)

| Calories: 390 | Carbohydrates: 944g | Fat: 23g | Protein: 9.4g |

117. Healthy Lemon Bars

Prep Time: 15 minutes

Cook Time: 15 minutes

Serves: 12

The healthiest lemon bars that are paleo, dairy-free, and gluten-free! The light lemon filling is prepared with just 4 basic ingredients, and the delectable shortbread crust is produced with a combination of almond and coconut flour. The ideal spring treat, these nutritious lemon bars are naturally sweetened.

For the crust:

- ¼ cup pure maple syrup
- 1/4 cup melted and cooled butter, melted coconut oil, or vegan butter
- ¼ teaspoon almond extract
- 2 tablespoons coconut flour
- 1 1/2 cups packed fine-blanched almond flour (do not use almond meal)
- 1/4 teaspoon salt

For the filling:

- 2/3 cup freshly squeezed lemon juice (from about 2-4 lemons)
- Zest from 1 lemon
- ½ cup pure maple syrup
- 1 tablespoon of coconut flour, sifted (or arrowroot starch or sub tapioca flour)
- 4 large eggs

To garnish:

- Lemon zest
- Powdered sugar (sifted)

1. Set the oven to 350 degrees Fahrenheit (1760C). Use parchment paper to line an 8x8-inch baking tray. (Avoid using a glass pan; the bottom of the crust will probably burn.)

2. Begin by making the crust by mixing the almond flour, salt, and coconut flour in a bowl. The butter, pure maple syrup, and almond essence are then added. Stir until a dough forms. Press the dough into the pan evenly with your hands. Bake for 15 minutes.

3. Prepare the filling in a bowl by whisking together the eggs, sifted coconut flour, pure maple syrup, lemon zest, and lemon juice while the crust bakes. To ensure that no egg white is left visible, whisk really well.

4. Immediately after the crust has finished baking, spoon the filling over it. It's crucial not to let the crust cool first.

5. Reduce the oven's temperature to 325 degrees F (1620C), put the bars in the oven right away, and bake them for 20 to 25 minutes, or until the filling is firm and does not jiggle any longer. Refrigerate for at least 4 hours to firm up the bars after thorough cooling on a wire rack. Cut the cake into 12 bars with a sharp knife when ready to serve. Before serving, I advise adding some lemon zest and powdered sugar as garnish. Enjoy!

NUTRITION FACTS (PER SERVING)

| Calories: 189 | Carbohydrates: 19g | Fat: 12g | Protein: 5g |

118. Torte Caprese (Italian Chocolate Cake)

Prep Time: 15 minutes

Cook Time: 30 minutes

Serves: 8

Beverage Paring: Pomegranate juice

Everyone can prepare this simple cake with little effort and basic ingredients. What makes me favor this cake is the consistency? The primary consistency is sort of crumbly because it isn't produced with flour and lacks dough as a result. But the flavor of chocolate and almonds, a match made in heaven, can be found in every crumbling piece. The very soft center contrasts with the slightly crispy exterior in terms of texture.

- 11 tbsps Unsalted butter at room temperature
- 5 ounces of Dark chocolate chips, 70% cacao minimum
- ⅔ cup Granulated sugar
- Confectioners' sugar
- 3 large Eggs at room temperature
- ¼ tsp Salt
- ¾ cup Almond flour

1. Set the oven to 350 degrees Fahrenheit (1760C). Butter or vegetable oil should be sprayed or brushed into the pan before lining the bottom of an 8- 10-inch cake pan with parchment paper.

2. Melt the chocolate either in the top section of a double boiler over simmering water or on low power in a microwave.

3. In another dish, combine the butter, sugar, and salt and use an electric mixer to thoroughly mix the ingredients.

4. Continue mixing after adding the eggs and almond flour to ensure that everything is thoroughly incorporated.

5. After letting the melted chocolate cool slightly, add it to the bowl and stir constantly until the batter is thoroughly combined and smooth.

6. Place the cake in the oven and bake for 25 to 30 minutes. The cake should not be overbaked because if it is, it will become too crumbly.

7. Let the cake cool in the pan before you remove it. Sprinkle confectioners' sugar over the cake, then serve it when it is at least 30 minutes cold.

NUTRITION FACTS (PER SERVING)

Calories: 450	Carbohydrates: 31g	Fat: 34g	Protein: 9g

119. Raw Vegan Brownie Bites

Prep Time: 15 minutes

Serves: 24

One of my all-time favorite treats is handmade energy balls, of which brownie bites are but one variation. Amazing things happen when nuts and dates are processed briefly in a food processor.

- 4 tablespoons cocoa powder or raw cacao, plus extra for rolling (if desired)
- 1 cup raw cashews or walnuts
- Generous pinch of sea salt
- 1 1/2 cups pitted, tightly packed Medjool dates
- 1/2 teaspoon vanilla extract (optional)

1. Use a food processor fitted with an S-shaped blade to grind the cashews, cacao powder, and sea salt. Process for about 30 seconds, or until the ingredients are quite thoroughly ground.

2. After adding the dates, run for an additional 1-2 minutes, or until the mixture comes together and is evenly blended. Squeezing a small amount of it in your hand should make it easily adhere together.

3. Roll the "dough" in your palms to form balls that are between 3/4 and 1 inch thick. If desired, add additional cacao or cocoa powder to a plate and coat the balls there.

4. Before serving, keep the energy bites in the refrigerator for 30 minutes. Enjoy!

NUTRITION FACTS (PER SERVING)

Calories: 430	Carbohydrates: 54g	Fat: 15g	Protein: 20g

120. Greek Almond Cookies

Prep Time: 15 minutes

Cook Time: 15 minutes

Serves: 36

Everyone can prepare this simple cake with little effort and basic ingredients. What makes me favor this cake is the consistency? The primary consistency is sort of crumbly because it isn't produced with flour and lacks dough as a result. But the flavor of chocolate and almonds, a match made in heaven, can be found in every crumbling piece. The very soft center contrasts with the slightly crispy exterior in terms of texture.

For the Dough

- 1 cup confectioners' sugar (7 ounces)
- 7 egg whites
- 24 ounces whole blanched almonds

For Topping the Cookies

- 2 ounces of whole-blanched almonds (about 36 almonds)
- rose water (optional)
- 3/4 cup confectioners' sugar
- 1 egg white

1. To make the dough, grind the almonds in a food processor until they resemble coarse sugar rather than fine flour.

2. Place the processed almonds in a sizable mixing bowl and combine them with the egg whites and confectioners' sugar.

3. Cover the dough with plastic and put it in the fridge for at least 30 minutes.

4. Place parchment paper on the baking sheets and preheat the oven to 300 degrees F.

5. Form 36 balls from 1-ounce chunks of dough. Roll the balls in sugar to decorate the cookies. One almond should be dipped in egg white and placed in the middle of a cookie. Continue by using the remaining almonds. You don't need to space the cookies too far apart because they won't spread out on the baking sheet while they bake.

Baking

1. Bake the cookies in the oven for 14 to 16 minutes or until the edges are just beginning to brown. When they first come out of the oven, they will be very mushy, but as they cool, they will start to keep their shape better. They can be baked for a little longer if you want a crispier cookie, although usually they are extremely soft.

2. Spray the cookies with rose water and top them with extra confectioners' sugar if you'd like.

NUTRITION FACTS (PER SERVING)

Calories: 164	Carbohydrates: 15g	Fat: 11g	Protein: 5g

BONUSES

The health benefits of mindful eating, which are sometimes underappreciated, are also acknowledged by the Mediterranean diet. Despite the fact that our schedules are often hectic, taking the time to prepare a meal at home and enjoy it might offer a number of unanticipated advantages over eating on the go or in front of the TV. We tend to be more aware of our hunger cues and how the food tastes when we eat without interruptions, making the meal more of an experience, and we consume fewer calories as a result.

YOUR 30-DAY MEDITERRANEAN DIET EATING PLAN

With a lot of meal-prep recipes and no-cook breakfast choices included in this 30-day meal plan, we've made eating healthy and losing weight possible for people with hectic schedules.

WEEK ONE

How to Prepare Your Meals for a Week?

1. Prepare the basil vinaigrette, transfer it to a meal-prep container (such as a Mason jar), and store it in the fridge for use over the course of the following week.
2. Prepare the Smoked Cheddar & Potato Muffin Tin Quiches to serve for breakfast on Days 2, 3, and 4. For later weeks' breakfast, individually wrap three servings in plastic and refrigerate them in an airtight bag. Take the separate portions in a small bag with you.
3. Prepare the Instant Pot White Chicken Chili Freezer Pack for Days 2, 3, 4, and 5's lunches. A big container, which is the ideal size for a 6-quart Instant Pot, can be used to freeze. After it has been cooked, divide the chili into 4 portions and freeze it in airtight containers for future weeks' lunches.

Day 1

Breakfast (297 calories)

- Pineapple Green Smoothie (1 serving)

Morning Snack (48 calories)

- 3/4 cup of raspberries

Lunch (375 calories)

- Tuna & Olive Spinach Salad (1 serving)

- 3/4 cup blackberries

Dinner (442 calories)

- Dijon Salmon with Green Bean Pilaf (1 serving)

Nutrition Facts (per serving)

1,209 calories

73 g protein

123 g carbohydrates

53 g fat

Day 2

Breakfast (238 calories)

- Muffin-Tin Quiches with Smoked Cheddar & Potato (1 serving)

Morning Snack (48 calories)

- 3/4 cup raspberries

Lunch (346 calories)

- 2 celery stalks
- White Chicken Chili Freezer Pack (1 serving)
- 3 Tbsp. hummus

Afternoon Snack (61 calories)

- 2 plums

Dinner (514 calories)

- Chicken & Vegetable Penne with Parsley-Walnut Pesto (1 serving)

Nutrition Facts (per serving)

1,206 calories

75 g protein

126 g carbohydrates

50 g fat

Day 3

Breakfast (238 calories)

- Muffin-Tin Quiches with Smoked Cheddar & Potato (1 serving)

Morning Snack (68 calories)

- 1 peach

Lunch (346 calories)

- 2 celery stalks
- White Chicken Chili Freezer Pack (1 serving)
- 3 Tbsp. hummus

Afternoon Snack (125 calories)

- 6 walnut halves
- 3/4 cup blackberries

Dinner (442 calories)

- 2 cups mixed greens
- Turkey Burgers with Spinach, Feta, and tzatziki (1 serving)
- 1 Tbsp. Basil Vinaigrette

Nutrition Facts (per serving)

1,219 calories

78 g protein

118 g carbohydrates

54 g fat

Day 4

Breakfast (238 calories)

- Muffin-Tin Quiches with Smoked Cheddar & Potato (1 serving)

Morning Snack (61 calories)

- 2 plums

Lunch (346 calories)

- 2 celery stalks
- White Chicken Chili Freezer Pack (1 serving)
- 3 Tbsp. hummus

Afternoon Snack (68 calories)

- 1 large peach

Dinner (500 calories)

- Meal-Prep Falafel Bowls with Tahini Sauce (1 serving)

Nutrition Facts (per serving)

1,213 calories

59 g protein

143 g carbohydrates

51 g fat

Day 5

Breakfast (297 calories)

- Pineapple Green Smoothie (1 serving)

Morning Snack (61 calories)

- 2 plums

Lunch (346 calories)

- White Chicken Chili Freezer Pack (1 serving)
- 3 Tbsp. hummus
- 2 celery stalks

Afternoon Snack (63 calories)

- 3/4 cup blueberries

Dinner (416 calories)

- Vegetarian Spaghetti Squash Lasagna (1 serving)
- 1 Tbsp. Basil Vinaigrette
- 2 cups mixed greens

Nutrition Facts (per serving)

1,183 calories

62 g protein

170 g carbohydrates

37 g fat.

Day 6

Breakfast (291 calories)

- Creamy Blueberry-Pecan Overnight Oatmeal (1 serving)

Morning Snack (48 calories)

- 3/4 cup raspberries

Lunch (375 calories)

- Tuna & Olive Spinach Salad (1 serving)

Afternoon Snack (46 calories)

- 3/4 cup blackberries

Dinner (443 calories)

- Hasselback Caprese Chicken (1 serving)
- Roasted Fresh Green Beans (1 ½ cups)

Nutrition Facts (per serving)

1,203 calories

77 g protein

116 g carbohydrates

55 g fat

Day 7

Breakfast (297 calories)

- Pineapple Green Smoothie (1 serving)

Morning Snack (61 calories)

- 2 plums

Lunch (375 calories)

- Tuna & Olive Spinach Salad (1 serving)

Afternoon Snack (16 calories)

- One cup sliced cucumbers with a squeeze of lemon juice, pepper, and salt to taste

Dinner (472 calories)

- Stuffed Sweet Potato with Hummus Dressing (1 serving)

Nutrition Facts (per serving)

1,221 calories

61 g protein

184 g carbohydrates

34 g fat

WEEK TWO

How to Prepare Your Meals for the Week:

1. To use throughout the week, prepare the Sheet-Pan Roasted Root Vegetables. To keep it fresh, store it in a sealed vessel.
2. Prepare the Basic Quinoa for usage over the course of the week. Use 1-half cups of quinoa and 3 cups of water or broth to increase the recipe to 6 cups. To keep it fresh, store it in a sealed vessel.
3. Prepare the herb dressing.
4. Prepare the Slow-Cooker Pasta e Fagioli Soup Freezer Pack for dinner on Day 11 and put it in a sizable freezer bag. On Day 10, during the night, move the freezer pack to the refrigerator so it can defrost.
5. Take one serving of the Smoked Cheddar and potato Muffin-Tin Quiches out of the freezer to eat for breakfast on Day 8. Remove the plastic wrap, wrap the food in a paper towel, and heat again in the microwave for 30 to 60 seconds.

Day 8

Breakfast (238 calories)

- Muffin-Tin Quiches with Smoked Cheddar & Potato (1 serving)

Morning Snack (16 calories)

- One cup sliced cucumber with a squeeze of lemon juice, pepper, and salt to taste

Lunch (472 calories)

- Stuffed Sweet Potato with Hummus Dressing (1 serving)

Afternoon Snack (30 calories)

- 1 plum

Dinner (453 calories)

- Roasted Root Veggies and greens over Spiced Lentils (1 serving)

Nutrition Facts (per serving)

1,209 calories

54 g protein

157 g carbohydrates

45 g fat

Day 9

Breakfast (291 calories)

- Creamy Blueberry-Pecan Overnight Oatmeal (1 serving)

Morning Snack (32 calories)

- 1/2 cup raspberries

Lunch (351 calories)

- Roasted Veggie and quinoa Salad (1 serving)

Afternoon Snack (8 calories)

- 1/2 cup sliced cucumber with a pinch of pepper and salt

Dinner (543 calories)

- One-Skillet Salmon with Fennel and sun-dried Tomato Couscous (1 serving)

Nutrition Facts (per serving)

1,225 calories

59 g protein

143 g carbohydrates

51 g fat

Day 10

Breakfast (250 calories)

- 1 hard-boiled egg
- Everything Bagel Avocado Toast (1 serving)

Morning Snack (64 calories)

- 1 cup raspberries

Lunch (351 calories)

- Roasted Veggie and quinoa Salad (1 serving)

Afternoon Snack (84 calories)

- 5 oz. Nonfat plain Greek yogurt

Dinner (479 calories)

- Chickpea and Quinoa Bowl with Roasted Red Pepper Sauce (1 serving)

Nutrition Facts (per serving)

1,227 calories

50 g protein

127 g carbohydrates

59 g fat

Day 11

Breakfast (287 calories)

- Muesli with Raspberries (1 serving)

Morning Snack (68 calories)

- 1 large peach

Lunch (351 calories)

- Roasted Veggie and quinoa Salad (1 serving)

Afternoon Snack (30 calories)

- 1 plum

Dinner (457 calories)

- Slow-Cooker Pasta e Fagioli Soup Freezer Pack (1 serving)

Nutrition Facts (per serving)

1,193 calories

59 g protein

158 g carbohydrates

44 g fat

Day 12

Breakfast (250 calories)

- 1 hard-boiled egg
- Everything Bagel Avocado Toast (1 serving)

Morning Snack (62 calories)

- 1 cup blackberries

Lunch (351 calories)

- Roasted Veggie and quinoa Salad (1 serving)

Afternoon Snack (181 calories)

- 1 Tbsp. chopped walnuts
- 1 cup nonfat plain Greek yogurt

Dinner (364 calories)

- 2 cups mixed greens
- No-Noodle Eggplant Lasagna (1 serving)
- 1 Tbsp. Herb Vinaigrette

Nutrition Facts (per serving)

1,206 calories

74 g protein

103 g carbohydrates

58 g fat

Day 13

Breakfast (287 calories)

- Muesli with Raspberries (1 serving)

Morning Snack (68 calories)

- 1 large peach

Lunch (301 calories)

- No-Noodle Eggplant Lasagna (1 serving)

Afternoon Snack (106 calories)

- 3 Tbsp. hummus
- 1 cup sliced red bell pepper

Dinner (446 calories)

- Slow-Cooker Chicken & Chickpea Soup (1 serving)

Nutrition Facts (per serving)

1,209 calories

77 g protein

143 g carbohydrates

40 g fat

Day 14

Breakfast (250 calories)

- 1 hard-boiled egg
- Everything Bagel Avocado Toast (1 serving)

Morning Snack (31 calories)

- 1/2 cup raspberries

Lunch (446 calories)

- Slow-Cooker Chicken & Chickpea Soup (1 serving)

Afternoon Snack (8 calories)

- 1/2 cup sliced cucumber with a pinch of pepper and salt

Dinner (487 calories)

- One-pot spinach, Chicken Sausage & Feta Pasta (1 serving)

Nutrition Facts (per serving)

1,224 calories

69 g protein

130 g carbohydrates

51 g fat

WEEK THREE

How to Prepare Your Meals for the Week

1. Prepare the Vegan Superfood Grain Bowls for Day 16, Day 17, Day 18, and Day 19's lunch. To it keep fresh for a week, store it in an airtight meal preparation container.
2. Prepare the parsley-lemon vinaigrette and serve it all week.
3. Take two portions of the Smoked Cheddar and potato Muffin-Tin Quiches out of the freezer to eat for breakfast on Days 17 and 19. Remove the packaging, cover it with a paper towel, and reheat on High for 30 to 60 seconds.

Day 15

Breakfast (291 calories)

- Creamy Blueberry-Pecan Overnight Oatmeal (1 serving)

Morning Snack (62 calories)

- 1 cup blackberries

Lunch (446 calories)

- Slow-Cooker Chicken and Chickpea Soup (1 serving)

Afternoon Snack (30 calories)

- 1 plum

Dinner (394 calories)

- 2 cups mixed greens
- Summer Shrimp Salad (1 serving)
- 1 Tbsp. Parsley-Lemon Vinaigrette

Nutrition Facts (per serving)

1,224 calories

77 g protein

127 g carbohydrates

49 g fat

Day 16

Breakfast (287 calories)

- Muesli with Raspberries (1 serving)

Morning Snack (8 calories)

- 1/2 cup sliced cucumbers with a pinch of pepper and salt

Lunch (381 calories)

- Vegan Superfood Grain Bowls (1 serving)

Afternoon Snack (14 calories)

- 1/2 cup sliced red bell pepper

Dinner (528 calories)

- Lemon Tahini Couscous with Chicken and Vegetables (1 serving)

Nutrition Facts (per serving)

1,219 calories

70 g protein

141 g carbohydrates

49 g fat

Day 17

Breakfast (238 calories)

- Muffin-Tin Quiches with Smoked Cheddar & Potato (1 serving)

Morning Snack (32 calories)

- 1/2 cup raspberries

Lunch (381 calories)

- Vegan Superfood Grain Bowls (1 serving)

Afternoon Snack (31 calories)

- 1/2 cup blackberries

Dinner (538 calories)

- Easy Brown Rice Pilaf with Spring Vegetables (1 serving)
- Walnut-Rosemary Crusted Salmon (1 serving)

Nutrition Facts (per serving)

1,219 calories

65 g protein

120 g carbohydrates

56 g fat

Day 18

Breakfast (274 calories)

- Berry-Mint Kefir Smoothies (2 servings)

Morning Snack (30 calories)

- 1 plum

Lunch (381 calories)

- Vegan Superfood Grain Bowls (1 serving)

Afternoon Snack (66 calories)

- 1/2 cup nonfat plain Greek yogurt

Dinner (460 calories)

- 1 Tbsp. Parsley-Lemon Vinaigrette
- Farfalle with Tuna, Lemon & Fennel (1 serving)
- 2 cups mixed greens

Nutrition Facts (per serving)

1,211 calories

59 g protein

155 g carbohydrates

45 g fat

Day 19

Breakfast (238 calories)

- Muffin-Tin Quiches with Smoked Cheddar & Potato (1 serving)

Morning Snack (30 calories)

- 1 plum

Lunch (381 calories)

- Vegan Superfood Grain Bowls (1 serving)

Afternoon Snack (105 calories)

- 1/4 cup blueberries
- 5 oz. Nonfat plain Greek yogurt

Dinner (472 calories)

- Cilantro Bean Burgers with Creamy Avocado-Lime Slaw (1 serving)
- 1 Tbsp. Parsley-Lemon Vinaigrette
- 2 cups mixed greens

Nutrition Facts (per serving)

1,226 calories

63 g protein

130 g carbohydrates

56 g fat

Day 20

Breakfast (274 calories)

- Berry-Mint Kefir Smoothies (2 servings)

Morning Snack (42 calories)

- 2/3 cup raspberries

Lunch (430 calories)

- Mason Jar Power Salad with Chickpeas and Tuna (1 serving)

Afternoon Snack (41 calories)

- 2/3 cup blackberries

Dinner (415 calories)

- Roasted Chicken & Winter Squash Over Mixed Greens (1 serving)

Nutrition Facts (per serving)

1,202 calories

72 g protein

142 g carbohydrates

42 g fat

Day 21

Breakfast (274 calories)

- Berry-Mint Kefir Smoothies (2 servings)

Morning Snack (32 calories)

- 1/2 cup raspberries

Lunch (430 calories)

- Mason Jar Power Salad with Chickpeas and Tuna (1 serving)

Afternoon Snack (31 calories)

- 1/2 cup blackberries

Dinner (443 calories)

- Sweet and Spicy Roasted Salmon with Wild Rice Pilaf (1 serving)
- 1 Tbsp. Parsley-Lemon Vinaigrette
- 2 cups mixed greens

Nutrition Facts (per serving)

1,210 calories

72 g protein

145 g carbohydrates

40 g fat

WEEK FOUR

How to Prepare Your Meals for the Week

1. To keep the roasted butternut squash and root vegetables fresh, prepare them and store them in the refrigerator in an airtight container.
2. To keep the Lemon-Roasted Mixed Vegetables fresh, cook them and place them in the refrigerator in an airtight container.
3. Prepare the Freezer Pack of Slow-Cooker Pasta e Fagioli Soup for Day 23's meal.

Day 22

Breakfast (297 calories)

- Pineapple Green Smoothie (1 serving)

Morning Snack (62 calories)

- 1 cup blackberries

Lunch (354 calories)

- 1 cup Roasted Butternut Squash and Root Vegetables
- 1 salmon fillet (left over from Sweet & Spicy Roasted Salmon with Wild Rice Pilaf)
- 1/3 cup Lemon-Roasted Mixed Vegetables

Afternoon Snack (68 calories)

- 1 large peach

Dinner (405 calories)

- Green Salad with Edamame and Beets (1 serving)
- 1/4 of an avocado

Nutrition Facts (per serving)

1,187 calories

63 g protein

151 g carbohydrates

42 g fat

Day 23

Breakfast (287 calories)

- Muesli with Raspberries (1 serving)

Morning Snack (30 calories)

- 1 plum

Lunch (399 calories)

- Piled-High Vegetable Pitas (1 serving)

Afternoon Snack (29 calories)

- 1 cup sliced red bell pepper

Dinner (457 calories)

- Slow-Cooker Pasta e Fagioli Soup Freezer Pack (1 serving)

Nutrition Facts (per serving)

1,202 calories

63 g protein

160 g carbohydrates

40 g fat

Day 24

Breakfast (250 calories)

- 1 hard-boiled egg
- Everything Bagel Avocado Toast (1 serving)

Morning Snack (42 calories)

- 2/3 cup raspberries

Lunch (399 calories)

- Piled-High Vegetable Pitas (1 serving)

Afternoon Snack (30 calories)

- 1 plum

Dinner (481 calories)

- Quinoa, Chicken, and Broccoli Salad with Roasted Lemon Dressing (1 serving)

Nutrition Facts (per serving)

1,202 calories

50 g protein

131 g carbohydrates

57 g fat

Day 25

Breakfast (229 calories)

- Blueberry Almond Chia Pudding (1 serving)

Morning Snack (153 calories)

- 1/4 cup blueberries
- 1 Tbsp. chopped walnuts
- 5 oz. Nonfat plain Greek yogurt

Lunch (399 calories)

- Piled-High Vegetable Pitas (1 serving)

Afternoon Snack (68 calories)

- 1 large peach

Dinner (364 calories)

- 3/4 cup Quinoa Avocado Salad
- Herby Cod with Roasted Tomatoes (1 serving)

Nutrition Facts (per serving)

1,213 calories

65 g protein

140 g carbohydrates

49 g fat

Day 26

Breakfast (250 calories)

- 1 hard-boiled egg
- Everything Bagel Avocado Toast (1 serving)

Morning Snack (64 calories)

- 1 cup raspberries

Lunch (399 calories)

- Piled-High Vegetable Pitas (1 serving)

Afternoon Snack (104 calories)

- 1/3 cup blackberries
- 5 oz. Nonfat plain Greek yogurt

Dinner (393 calories)

- Caprese Stuffed Portobello Mushrooms (1 serving) with 3/4 cup Quinoa Avocado Salad

Nutrition Facts (per serving)

1,210 calories

54 g protein

124 g carbohydrates

60 g fat

Day 27

Breakfast (287 calories)

- Muesli with Raspberries (1 serving)

Morning Snack (68 calories)

- 1 large peach

Lunch (298 calories)

- 1/2 cup blueberries
- White Chicken Chili Freezer Pack (1 serving)

Afternoon Snack (47 calories)

- 1 Tbsp. hummus
- 3/4 cup sliced red bell pepper

Dinner (513 calories)

- Traditional Greek Salad (1 serving)
- Stuffed Eggplant (1 serving)

Nutrition Facts (per serving)

1,214 calories

54 g protein

157 g carbohydrates

49 g fat

Day 28

Breakfast (274 calories)

- Berry-Mint Kefir Smoothies (2 servings)

Morning Snack (14 calories)

- 1/2 cup sliced red bell pepper

Lunch (298 calories)

- 1/2 cup blueberries
- Pot White Chicken Chili Freezer Pack (1 serving)

- 1/2 cup sliced cucumbers with a pinch of pepper and salt

Dinner (630 calories)

- Chickpea Pasta with Lemony-Parsley Pesto (1 serving)

Nutrition Facts (per serving)

1,224 calories

53 g protein

154 g carbohydrates

50 g fat

WEEK FIVE

How to Prepare Your Meals for the Week

1. To enjoy breakfast on Day 30, prepare 1 serving of Blueberry Almond Chia Pudding and store it in a leak-proof container.
2. Defrost 2 portions of the Instant Pot White Chicken Chili Freezer Pack in the refrigerator for lunch on Days 29 and 30, if you haven't already.

Day 29

Breakfast (250 calories)

- 1 hard-boiled egg
- Everything Bagel Avocado Toast (1 serving)

Morning Snack (108 calories)

- 5 walnut halves
- 2/3 cup fresh raspberries

Lunch (298 calories)

- 1/2 cup blueberries
- White Chicken Chili Freezer Pack (1 serving)

Afternoon Snack (132 calories)

- 7 walnut halves
- 2/3 cup blackberries

Dinner (422 calories)

- Sheet-Pan Roasted Salmon and Vegetables (1 serving)

Nutrition Facts (per serving)

1,210 calories

74 g protein

119 g carbohydrates

53 g fat

Day 30

Breakfast (229 calories)

- Blueberry Almond Chia Pudding (1 serving)

Morning Snack (68 calories)

- 1 large peach

Lunch (298 calories)

- 1/2 cup blueberries
- White Chicken Chili Freezer Pack (1 serving)

Afternoon Snack (157 calories)

- 12 walnut halves

Dinner (450 calories)

- Cucumber, Tomato, and Avocado Salad (1 serving)
- Slow-Cooker Chicken & Orzo with Tomatoes and Olives (1 serving)

Nutrition Facts (per serving)

1,201 calories

66 g protein

138 g carbohydrates

49 g fat

CONVERSION TABLE

Conversion tables for volume and weight are a useful tool to have in the kitchen. Making the right conversions can make or break your results when halfing or doubling a recipe.

The following table provides a brief summary of conversions:

Tablespoons	Teaspoons	Cups	Ounces	Quartz	Pints	Gallons	Liters	Milliliters
1	3	1/16	½				15	0.015
4	12	¼	2				60	0.06
8	24	½	4				125	0.125
16	48	1	8	1/4	½	1/16	250	0.25
		2	16	½	1	1/8	500	0.5
		4	32	1	2	¼	950	0.95
		16	128	4	8	1	3800	0.38

CONCLUSION

Adopting the tasty and healthful Mediterranean diet can improve your general health and well-being. You'll quickly start living a healthy lifestyle if you adhere to this guide's advice and meal suggestions.

It's understandable why dishes for the Mediterranean diet have been popular for so long. This diet strongly emphasizes fruits, vegetables, whole grains, nuts, and meals high in protein like fish and healthy fats like olive oil. Another benefit of the Mediterranean diet is that the dishes are inherently salt-free. Although there is a lot of debate about which foods should be considered part of a Mediterranean diet, one thing that everyone agrees on is that it's best to eat as many unprocessed or minimally processed ingredients as you can while avoiding meats raised with antibiotics, hormones, or pesticides; basically, eating whole food versions of your favorite dishes! That is something I believe we can all support!

THANK YOU FOR READING!

I've thoroughly enjoyed writing this book and sincerely hope you've found it valuable and enjoyable. If you have, it would be greatly appreciated if you could take a moment to **leave a review** on Amazon!

Your reviews greatly support small publishers like myself. Reader feedback lets me know how I've done and what I can improve on to serve you on my next book!

Simply scan the **QR code** with your phone, and you will be directed to the book's review page.

Alternatively, to leave a review:
- Visit the book's page on Amazon or find it through your purchases.
- Scroll down to the bottom of the page and click on the button that says "Write a Customer Review".
- You can simply leave a star rating out of 5, or write a short review!

Thank You! Your support is greatly appreciated!

Made in United States
Troutdale, OR
06/04/2024

The
MEDITERRANEAN
DIET *Made Simple*

Are you tired of trendy diets that leave you hungry and unsatisfied? Yearning for a sustainable change? Look nowhere else! This book is your ticket to a vibrant, Mediterranean-inspired lifestyle. Here's what you'll find inside:

120 Simple, Healthy Recipes: Dive into a collection of straightforward, tried-and-tested, and delicious dishes. Created with fresh, wholesome ingredients, each recipe includes detailed nutrition information for effortless enjoyment.

Effortless Meal Solutions: Say goodbye to meal prep worries. Our 30-day meal plan empowers you to effortlessly weave the Mediterranean diet into your daily routine, even on the busiest days.

Simplicity Unleashed: Bid farewell to decision overwhelm. This book simplifies your journey to a healthier lifestyle, presenting accessible, enriching recipes that turn every meal into a mindful step towards well-being.

Cooking Made Easy: Benefit from straightforward cooking instructions that make preparing nutritious and delicious meals a breeze.

Embark on a transformative journey within the pages of "The Mediterranean Diet Made Simple." From practical tips to seasonal delights, savour the richness of the Mediterranean way of life, your adventure starts here.

HAPPY HEALTH HAVE

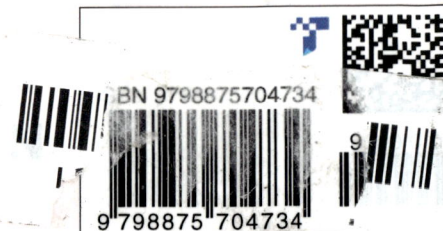

BN 9798875704734

9798875704734